Off Grid Solar
A Handbook for Photovoltaics with Lead-Acid or Lithium-Ion Batteries

Joseph P. O'Connor

Cover Design by Jean-Baptiste Vervaeck

ISBN 978-0-578-54619-3 (English Paperback)
ISBN 978-1-7334543-0-8 (English eBook)
ISBN 978-1-7334543-1-5 (Spanish Paperback)
ISBN 978-1-7334543-2-2 (Spanish eBook)

Old Sequoia Publishing
www.OffGridSolarBook.com

First Edition: November 2016
Second Edition: August 2019

DEDICATION

This book would not have happened without you, Jessica.
Thank you for all your support and encouragement.

Table of Contents

About the Author

Joe O'Connor is a solar manufacturing entrepreneur as well as a consultant, speaker, and writer on solar energy. Joe has built off grid solar energy systems in the U.S., Haiti, Nepal, Portugal, Guatemala, and most recently in Virunga National Park, Democratic Republic of the Congo. To learn more about his work in Congo, check out *SolarCity, Tesla, and Virunga, Building Solar Micro Grids for the guardians of Africa's oldest and most biodiverse national park.*

Seeking to amplify his impact after over a decade of traveling to remote places to install solar, Joe decided to share his knowledge and experience of off grid solar energy systems through this book.

As founder of OCON Energy Consulting, Joe and his team provide consulting services for a range of clients in need of solar system design, energy storage systems, and product development.

Joe currently works at Nuvation Energy, providing battery management technology and engineering services to organizations designing and building energy storage systems.

Joe has worked at lithium-ion battery manufacturer Farasis Energy, energy storage provider Mercedes-Benz Energy, and solar installer SolarCity. At SolarCity, Joe supported the Microgrid Team and the GivePower Foundation by designing solar photovoltaic and Tesla Powerwall systems. He also prototyped, designed, and patented a new solar racking system that enabled SolarCity to become one of the largest commercial installers in the U.S.

Prior to his work at SolarCity, Joe launched a cost-efficient solar racking product at solar manufacturing start-up, Sollega. Joe has also worked with Sustainable Energy Partners in San Francisco, completing dozens of renewable energy and energy efficiency projects.

Joe earned his M.S. from NYU Polytechnic University in Manufacturing Engineering and was selected as a recipient of the Catherine B. Reynolds Foundation Fellowship for Social Entrepreneurship. He earned his B.S. from Cal Poly University in Industrial Technology.

He first became passionate about renewable energy after volunteering with GRID Alternatives—the Habitat for Humanities of the solar industry—when he teamed up with other volunteers to install solar electric systems on homes of low-income families in the San Francisco Bay Area.

Joe believes that advancements in the renewable energy industry will help our global society break its dependency on oil, coal, and natural gas. He is on a mission to make renewables the dominant energy sources on our planet in order to combat climate change.

More Resources

At the website below there are more resources available to assist in the design of an off grid solar system. These resources are free for download:
- System Designer template in MS Excel
    - Load calculator table
    - Derate Table
    - System Summary
- Bill of Materials template in MS Excel
- Solar insolation maps
- Declination maps
- Voltage drop calculator
- GOGLA *Photovoltaics for Productive Use Applications: A Catalogue of DC-Appliances.*

Visit the following link for more information or to contact the author.

www.OffGridSolarBook.com

Disclaimer

All content in this book is provided for educational purposes and should be applied at your own risk. As with any Do-It-Yourself (DIY) project, unfamiliarity with tools and processes can be dangerous. All content herein should be considered theoretical advice only.

If you are at all uncomfortable or inexperienced working with the components and/or tools required for off grid solar systems (especially but not limited to electronics and mechanical equipment), please reconsider doing the job yourself. It is very possible on any DIY project to damage the equipment, void property insurance, create a hazardous condition, or harm or even kill yourself or others.

The author and this book are not to be held responsible for any injury due to the misuse or misunderstanding of any content related to this book.

By using this book, you agree to indemnify the author ("The Company"), its officers, directors, employees, agents, distributors, affiliates, subsidiaries and their related companies for any and all claims, damages, losses and causes of action arising out of your breach or alleged breach of this agreement.

The information in this book is distributed "as is" and appears without express or implied warranties of any kind, except those required by the relevant legislation. In particular the Company makes no warranty as to the accuracy, quality, completeness or applicability of the information provided.

You may not rely on any information and opinions expressed in it for any other purpose. Neither the Company, nor its officers, directors, employees, agents, distributors, affiliates, subsidiaries and their related companies are responsible or liable for any loss damage (including, but not limited to, actual, consequential, or punitive), liability, claim, or any other injury or cause related to or resulting from any information in this book or on the Company's website.

"If we use our fuel to get our power, we are living on our capital and exhausting it rapidly. This method is barbarous and wantonly wasteful, and will have to be stopped in the interest of coming generations."

– Nikola Tesla, 1915

"I'd put my money on the sun and solar energy. What a source of power! I hope we don't have to wait until oil and coal run out before we tackle that. I wish I had more years left!"

– Thomas Edison, 1931

Introduction

Are you planning to build an off grid solar energy system? Maybe you don't feel quite ready and want support in understanding the technology and the process? This book is written so that you can decide the best equipment for your project, matching your particular needs within a realistic budget. After reading this book, you will have a firm understanding of how photovoltaic solar panels and batteries work together to provide DC or AC electricity in an off grid environment.

First, I will explain the basics of the solar components and the general science behind solar electric systems. Next, I will help you determine how much power and energy can be produced in a particular location and which combination of equipment will match your load at the lowest cost. Finally, I will explain the specifics of the installation process and conclude with a section on how to troubleshoot problems.

By the time you've finished reading, you will be capable of building your own off grid solar system, assuming you have the right tools as well as some construction and electrical skills and experience. This book will help you make better decisions about solar. You'll understand what technology you truly need, rather than solely trusting others for recommendations. You'll be better at comparing bids from installers because you will recognize which technology best suits the needs of your project.

Whenever possible in this book, I have avoided recommending specific manufacturers. I choose to remain technologically agnostic, so you can determine the right *specifications* rather than specific brands in your decision-making process. It is up to you to decide what level of quality you need. For your system to last a long time, make sure the products you purchase have long warranties from reputable manufacturers.

This book is geared toward people who want an off grid electric energy system, one that is self-sufficient and does not require access to a shared grid. It is designed for people who lack a reliable utility or who wish to avoid one that relies on expensive and dirty fossil fuels. This book covers systems both large and small, and it will be useful whether you need to power a few lights and cell phone chargers at a low cost, or need to power every appliance in your home. There is a clear comparison between today's tried-and-true lead-acid batteries and tomorrow's lithium-ion batteries. This book will also be suitable for someone building a remote energy source for research or communications equipment.

There are many similarities between off grid and grid-tied solar energy systems; this book focuses *only* on the needs of a stand-alone energy system. People living in cities or suburbs connected to a reliable utility grid may find this book interesting as well, but its guidance may not apply to grid-tied systems, which often require different components and are generally less complex, as there is no need to store energy. There are already many great resources focusing on grid-tied PV systems, such as the *NABCEP PV Installation Professional Resource Guide*.

If your project can be grid-tied, it generally should be grid-tied, since feeding the grid is more efficient than storing it in batteries, and because someone will use the extra electricity somewhere on the grid. However, in some places such as in Germany and Hawaii, solar owners are not allowed to export onto the grid because there is a surplus of electricity on the grid during the hours of intense sunshine. This is a new issue and will become more common as solar becomes ubiquitous. However, in those areas where solar energy cannot be exported, homeowners and businesses are using lithium-ion batteries to store their solar energy for use at later times.

Off grid solar is the ideal form of self-reliance. With solar energy you don't need to pay bills to a utility or buy an endless supply of fuel for your generator; you can harvest energy from the sky. By avoiding dirty fossil fuels, you also avoid contributing to climate change. The technology is here, so let's get started and learn how to use it.

Why Solar?

To me, the most interesting fact about solar is that there is no cost for the fuel — unlike fossil fuels. This means that as the cost to manufacture solar equipment continues to decrease, solar will quickly become the cheapest energy source on the planet. In fact, it is already the cheapest form of energy in many regions of the world. Yet despite this, many people globally still live without access to energy.

"The 1.2 billion people living without access to the power grid spend about $27 billion annually on lighting and mobile-phone charging with kerosene, candles, battery torches or other fossil-fuel powered stopgap technologies.

About 1-in-3 off-grid households globally will use off-grid solar by 2020, according to our baseline forecast."

— Off-Grid Solar Market Trends Report 2016, Bloomberg New Energy Finance and Lighting Global.

In 2013, the World Bank stated that over 1.4 billion people have no access to electricity worldwide—almost all in developing countries. This includes about 550 million in Africa, and over 400 million in India. Access to energy can be expensive if one is not located near a utility grid. Dirty fuels such as diesel, kerosene, and charcoal have historically been the easiest energy sources, because until recently there weren't good alternatives. Now that has changed, thanks to solar technology.

In many markets, the cost of electricity from diesel is $0.28 per kWh and the cost to use kerosene for lighting is equivalent to $3.00 per kWh. Solar energy is already significantly cheaper than current energy sources and, in some markets, is quickly replacing dirty fuels as an energy source.

What is so great about solar anyways?

1. It is *by far* the most abundant energy source on our planet. (see figure below)
2. It is cost effective at all scales—large and small.
3. The cost of fuel is free!

EARTH'S TOTAL ENERGY RESOURCES

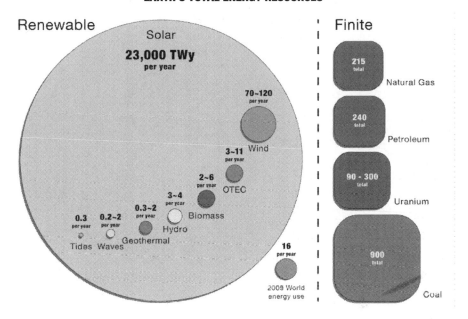

Cost of Solar

Historically solar has been very expensive. In the 1950s, when the solar photovoltaic cell was first invented by Bell Labs, it was so expensive that it wasn't even considered a viable energy source unless you were designing a satellite for outer space. Fossil fuel was the most versatile and inexpensive source of energy. Hydroelectric dams were an inexpensive renewable option, but they were and still are extremely dependent on regional resources, and can damage surrounding natural ecosystems.

COST OF SOLAR PV OVER TIME

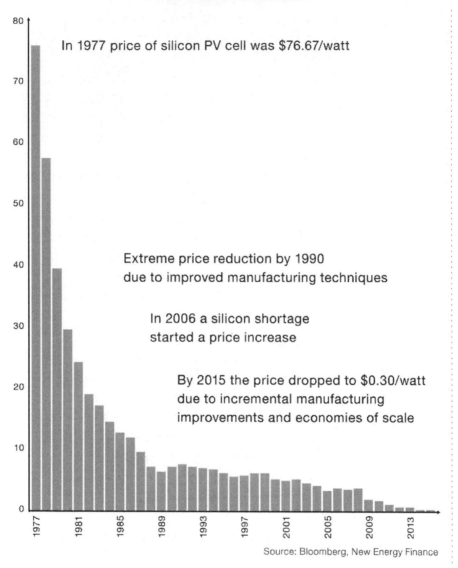

In 1977 price of silicon PV cell was $76.67/watt

Extreme price reduction by 1990
due to improved manufacturing techniques

In 2006 a silicon shortage
started a price increase

By 2015 the price dropped to $0.30/watt
due to incremental manufacturing
improvements and economies of scale

Source: Bloomberg, New Energy Finance

Fossil fuel costs have fluctuated radically over time and the average prices over the long-term have been increasing. For decades we have built substantial global infrastructure around fossil fuels. Our economy currently depends on it, and it is difficult to change this infrastructure until alternatives to fossil fuels become extremely cost effective, to recoup the sunk cost.

But the compound negative effects on our environment along with a growing scarcity of supply—and thus, increasing costs—makes the transition away from fossil fuels inevitable.

Luckily, we now have a viable, cost-effective renewable energy source: solar. The cost of solar has dropped over 100 times since its invention decades ago. Since fuel is free with solar, there is less risk of price spikes in the market.

Many regions have already reached the tipping point where solar is the most cost-effective energy source. For example, a solar lamp in the developing world costs $0.26 per kWh compared to the previously-stated $3.00 per kWh cost of a kerosene lamp. In fact, a well maintained off grid solar PV system could drop costs to as low as just $0.20 per kWh compared to the previously-stated $0.28 per kWh for diesel generators.

The current limitations to widespread solar are not centered on cost, efficiency, or a need for advancements in technology. The limitations are mostly due to a lack of widespread knowledge on the subject. Once this knowledge achieves greater ubiquity, the materials can be better distributed. It's just a matter of time until the rest of the world favors solar for the reduced cost of energy, not to mention that it's a clear solution toward combating climate change.

Why then, if the technology is so inexpensive and readily available, hasn't solar had mass adoption?

Solar equipment is complicated to manufacture and therefore is centrally made and distributed around the world. The equipment is bulky and fragile, so it can be a costly mistake if it gets damaged in transport or is used improperly after installation. Also, it is fairly difficult to distribute solar equipment to a foreign country. In many developing countries getting through customs is a dreadful process filled with long delays, fees, and even bribes. The process is only slightly better when people within the country import solar products to sell within their community, but they typically pay much more for lower quality products compared to countries with established trade agreements.

As solar equipment becomes more commonly distributed as a traded good, it will become less expensive and of higher quality. Solar hasn't yet dominated electricity grids, but the solar revolution has certainly begun. In fact, I have seen solar equipment in almost every remote village I've ever visited. The equipment I saw wasn't particularly high quality, name brand, or the newest technology, but it was plentiful and seemed functional in most cases. In Nebaj, a remote town in Guatemala, the hardware store sold many sizes of solar panels and deep cycle batteries, but did not have charge controllers. Deep in the Congo I saw a store selling solar panels, batteries, and musical instruments — the essentials to life!

Regardless of quality, this equipment is already making its way to remote villages far from original manufacturing sites. That is amazing evidence that off grid solar technology is primed to propagate around the planet, electrifying the world's remote villages far from the grid.

SOLAR STORE IN KIWANJA, DEMOCRATIC REPUBLIC OF THE CONGO

Get Pumped! Solar Is Our Future

Solar energy is free! The technology available for sale today can be used to build a sustainable energy infrastructure in our immediate future. Today, as a global community, we have the knowledge and resources to live a life without fossil fuels. Whether you want to reduce your dependency on fossil fuels, live a life disconnected from the grid, or reduce your impact on climate change, solar is the technology that will get you there.

With 378,000 km² of solar PV, or approximately 4% of the land area of the Sahara Desert, we could produce enough energy to fulfill the entire global demand for electricity. That's with today's PV technology, not something futuristic or theoretical. When you think of the area of the planet that we've already paved with roads, covered with buildings, or developed for farming, using a small amount of that space for solar PV is not unrealistic. This fact alone convinces me that solar energy is not just exciting, but is the only logical solution for a sustainable future.

AREA REQUIRED TO MEET GLOBAL ELECTRICITY DEMAND

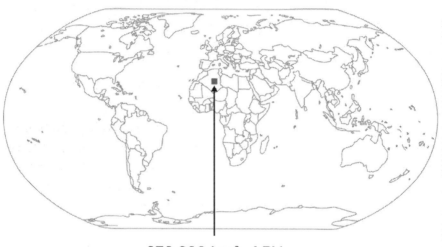

378,000 km² of PV

The 378,000 km² of solar PV can generate 16 terawatt-years of energy that would cover all electrical consumption, all machinery, and all forms of transportation, based on the US Department of Energy statistics of worldwide consumption.

How Off Grid Solar Works

The Sun (Fuel Source)

With a solar power system, you never need to purchase fuel; it is wirelessly transmitted from a fusion reactor safely placed 149.6 million kilometers away. The sunlight that hits Earth is equivalent to 170,000,000 gigawatts of power, and, in just eight minutes, enough energy reaches our planet's surface to meet global electricity needs for an entire year. The sun is the most abundant fuel source available to us. Thanks to technology developed in the past 50 years, sunlight is now incredibly easy to capture.

Solar Panel (Sunlight to Electricity Converter)

Photovoltaic (PV) solar cells convert the sun's flying photons into an electrical charge. Photons from the sun hit electrons on the top layer of the PV cell, pushing them through a boundary layer where they end up on the back side of the cell. The electrons want to return to where they came from, so they rush back to the front of the cell through the path of least resistance. This electron movement is what creates power in the solar panel.

BASIC COMPONENTS FOR OFF GRID SOLAR

SUN
FUEL SOURCE

SOLAR PANEL
*SUNLIGHT TO
ELECTRICITY CONVERTER*

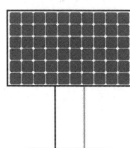

CHARGE CONTROLLER
ENERGY MANAGER

BATTERY
ENERGY CONTAINER

INVERTER
ENERGY CONVERTER

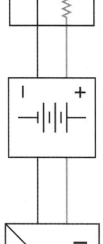

Charge Controller (Energy Manager)

Charge Controllers protect the battery and optimize the energy coming from the solar panels. Like a police officer directing traffic in an intersection, Charge Controllers decide how energy flows based on a set of rules. The electronics inside are designed to only let electricity flow under specific conditions and to protect the batteries. Some Charge Controllers also alter the voltage to optimize performance.

Battery (Energy Container)

Batteries store and contain electrical potential in the form of chemical bonds. The chemicals separate inside the battery so the positively and negatively charged molecules are stored in opposite sides of the battery. Once the molecules are reunited, an opportunity to produce electrical energy is created. There are many types of batteries with different chemistries, but they function under the same principle that the chemical bonds hold or release an electric charge.

Inverter (Energy Converter)

Inverters "invert" direct current (DC) energy into alternating current (AC). They can also change the voltage. In off grid solar, they invert the DC power coming from the batteries and the solar panels into AC power. Not all off grid energy systems require an inverter; they are only needed if some of the equipment runs on AC.

Site Design

Before you can install a solar energy system you need to first understand what needs power, when it's needed, and how much daily energy is required. For any off grid solar energy system, you must work backward starting with your site's energy needs, so that the equipment works for you and not the other way around. This section will help you determine how your site uses power and energy and how much solar energy is available to you.

We first need to consider the difference between power and energy, since people sometimes mistakenly use the words "power" and "energy" interchangeably. Power is an instantaneous rate and is the ratio of energy per unit of time. By contrast, energy is the amount of power that is generated or consumed over a period of time. For example, let's consider a bucket of water. The rate at which you pour out the water is like power: if you pour it out slow, low power; if you pour it out fast, high power. And the amount of water in the bucket is the energy. Solar panels produce *power* when exposed to sunlight, and batteries store *energy*.

If you are not familiar with energy systems or electrical engineering then you might be confused by the units used to quantify power (**watts**) and energy (**watt-hours**). A watt-hour is not a ratio; not watts per hour, but rather, one watt times one hour. For a more detailed description of energy and power see the *Understanding Electricity* chapter at the end of the book.

Start With Energy Efficiency

The most cost effective solar energy system is the smallest system you need. Before designing your system, first think about your energy needs. What do you really need to power? What is essential? If five TVs, a huge air-conditioning system, hot tub, and an extravagant water fountain display is essential, that's great, but you'll need a much larger solar energy system.

Avoid designing your solar energy system for outdated and inefficient equipment. For example, it is worth it to buy new, efficient light bulbs even if you have old, inefficient ones that haven't yet burned out. Spending money on energy efficiency is usually cheaper than buying a larger solar energy system. Investing in LED lights or a high-efficiency refrigerator will almost always cost less than running inefficient equipment with a larger solar system. But don't just take my word for it; you should do the calculations yourself.

Load Calculation Table

Take an inventory of all the equipment using electricity that you plan to power with your solar energy system by making a **Load Calculation Table,** which is simply a spreadsheet listing each appliance's running wattage, average daily hours of use, and whether or not it is essential. The wattage is typically listed on the nameplate of the appliance along with the serial number and product specifications. If you cannot figure out the wattage, use a Kill A Watt meter to measure the running wattage. See the Tools section in the *System Design* chapter to learn more about Kill A Watt meters.

Here is an example of a load calculation table with 4 LED lights, 2 cell phone chargers, a fan, and a TV.

EXAMPLE OF A LOAD CALCULATION TABLE

Appliance	Running Wattage (W)	AVG Daily Usage (hours)	Total Energy Watt-hours (Wh)	Essential?
4 LED lights	20w × 4 = 80	6	480	Y
Charging for 2 Cell phones	10w × 2 = 20	2	40	Y
Fan	100	4	400	Y
LCD TV	150	2	300	N
Essentials	80+20+100 = 200		480+40+400 = 920	
Nonessentials	150		300	
TOTAL	350		1220 Wh	

Peak Power   **= 200 watts**
Daily Energy Usage **= 1,220 watt-hours**

Peak power and daily energy usage are the two important values you must gain from the load calculation table. **Peak power** is the maximum load of only the essential appliances that could function at the same time. If all appliances are essential then you can remove this column or mark everything as essential. If you are trying to save on equipment costs then you can mark some of these items as not essential, and in doing so, plan to only use those nonessential appliances when there is enough power available. **Daily energy usage** is the energy usage under normal conditions.

Peak Power

The above load calculation table is used to add up the running wattage of all the essential equipment that could run at the same time. The most power you may need at any given time is called the **peak power** of your system. You may determine that all your loads are essential, but in some cases you can take some equipment off the essential list. Find the running wattage of all your devices and determine under which circumstances the most power will be used at a single moment.

In the example on the previous page, 200 watts is the peak power, so you would need to purchase an inverter with a capacity of at least 200 watts if you only use your TV when your lights and fan are off. In this case, it would be pretty easy to turn off the nonessential equipment, and you could save on your equipment costs

Start-up or Surge Power

Sometimes appliances have a **start-up** or **surge** wattage that is larger than the running wattage. Also known as **inrush current**, a surge occurs when certain electrical equipment is first turned on and additional current flows that exceeds the steady-state running current. Appliances with power converters, motors, and transformers all have a start-up surge. Well pumps, for example, have a motor driving the turbine in the pump. All motors create a spike in power in the first few seconds as the motor accelerates, then it reduces to the running wattage once it has reached a steady speed. There are many types of motors, all with different levels of inrush current. Larger motors have a defined inrush current that can be calculated based on the code letter shown on its nameplate. The surge power can be three or four times the running wattage, so keep this in mind if you plan to use any large motors or equipment that uses motors. Camera flashes have large capacitors with a large inrush current. Surge Power cannot be measured with a regular multimeter or a Kill A Watt meter. However, some clamp meters have an inrush current setting that can measure peak current.

If you are using equipment that has a significant surge you should add a column to the load calculation table. Determine the one appliance that has the largest surge, then add up all of the wattages of the essential loads and add only the largest surge wattage. This is the peak surge power. An inverter will usually have a peak surge capacity that is larger than its running capacity, so you will need to determine if the inverter you are using will work with your equipment's running wattage as well as its surge wattage.

EXAMPLE OF A LOAD CALCULATION TABLE WITH SURGE

Appliance	Running Wattage (W)	Surge Wattage (W)	AVG Daily Usage (hours)	Total Energy Watt-hours (Wh)	Essential?
4 LED lights	80	-	6	480	Y
Charging for 2 cell phones	20	-	2	40	Y
Fan	100	200	4	400	N
LCD TV	150	-	2	300	N
Water pump	500	1500	0.5	250	Y
Essentials	80 + 20 + 500 = **600**	80 + 20 + 1500 = **1600**		480 + 40 + 250 = 770	
Nonessentials	250			700	
TOTAL	850			**1470**	

Using the example above, let's assume you add a water pump and it has a surge of 1500 watts. The load calculation table would look like this:

Peak Continuous Power = **600 watts**
Peak Surge Power = **1,600 watts**
Daily Energy Usage = **1,470 watt-hours**

By adding the pump, the Daily Energy Usage is only slightly higher, so this system could use the same battery capacity as the first example. However, the **Peak Surge Power** increased significantly, so it will need an inverter capable of handling a 1,600-watt surge. It is helpful to note both the **Peak Power** and **Peak Surge Power**, because most inverters have a continuous and surge power rating. Making a load calculation table is important because the most cost-effective off grid energy system is one that is designed and optimized for its own specific load profile.

Phantom Power

Some products, like televisions and cell phone chargers, use energy when they are plugged in even when the devices themselves are turned off. Sometimes this is called standby power, phantom power, or vampire power. These products use a little bit of energy to power internal electronics such as an internal clock. It may seem insignificant, but a few watts will add up quickly if appliances stay plugged in 24 hours a day. For example, if you use a TV for an hour per day and it consumes 150 watts when it's on and 5 watts when it's off, then you will use $150\,W \times 1\,hr = 150\,Wh$ when it's on and $5\,W \times 23\,hr = 115\,Wh$ when it's off. That's almost half of the total energy consumed while it's off!

I recommend using a surge protector with an on/off switch to completely turn off equipment with phantom power. Otherwise, account for the phantom power as another row in the load calculation table, or else plan on manually unplugging equipment with phantom power. Even the inverter used with your batteries will use some amount of power, which is usually called standby or idle power.

High-Power Equipment

Not all electrical devices are created equal; some appliances require 100x more power than others. For example, an LED light bulb uses fewer than 10 watts, but a toaster uses 1500 watts. The largest energy hogs, such as air conditioners, refrigerators, electric heaters, welders, and large motors, could use more energy in a few hours than your lights would use in a whole year! If you need to use high-powered equipment, make sure you plan your system size accordingly so that the batteries and inverter can handle the high current.

Daily Energy Requirements

Some equipment, like lighting, requires power for over 8 hours a day, while a device like a toaster might only be on for a few minutes a day. Lighting typically requires low power, but with longer use may consume more energy overall. If you infrequently use some equipment, then take the daily average over a week. In some cases you might want to err on the safe side and overestimate. For example, in the winter you might use your lights for a longer period of time than in the summer.

Days of Autonomy

Now that you know the average daily energy requirements, you might want to size your battery capacity for more than just one day's worth of energy needs. **Days of Autonomy** are the number of days the fully charged batteries can meet the system load requirements without recharging. Solar energy can decrease significantly in the winter months, and cloud cover might reduce your energy production enough that your batteries may not get completely charged even after a full day. If you have a secondary energy source like wind, hydro, or a backup generator, then you may not need more than one or two days of autonomy. See the *Secondary Power Selection* chapter for more details. However, if you are off grid with no other energy source, then you might want up to three days of autonomy. Choosing three days of autonomy will certainly prolong the life of your batteries, but it is a very costly decision. You could also opt to reduce your energy usage when the batteries are low on energy.

Site Location

With a load calculation table and understanding of your unique energy needs, you can now start to determine how much solar energy is available to harvest in your particular area. Solar geometry and the location of the sun can be challenging, but are essential factors, as the amount of sunlight varies depending on your location on the planet.

Sun Position

The location of the sun is commonly measured by two angles. The **azimuth angle** measures the sun's location as it changes throughout the day, from when it rises in the east to when it sets in the west. The azimuth is similar to how a sundial measures the time of the day. In the morning the sun's azimuth is a positive value, at noon it is zero, and in the evening it is a negative value.

The second angle used to measure the Sun is the **altitude**. This is the measurement of how high the sun is above the horizon and depends on the season and your latitude. The Earth's axis is tilted compared to the path it takes around the sun, so in the wintertime you'll notice that the altitude of the sun is lower than in the summer. The summer and winter solstice define the maximum and minimum solar altitude. The angle is measured in degrees with the horizon being zero and directly overhead being 90 degrees. If you live north of the Tropic of Cancer or south of the Tropic of Capricorn, the sun will never reach 90 degrees altitude. If you live within the Tropic of Cancer and the Tropic of Capricorn, i.e., near the equator, then the sun will be directly overhead (at 90 degrees) twice a year.

Sun Path

It is helpful to visualize the sun path throughout the year. First, start by imagining a trip to the equator during the spring or fall equinox. Turn to look directly east for the sunrise. The sun will rise directly in front of you, rise to a point directly overhead and set directly behind you, as if it was a straight line over your body. Now, imagine you walked directly north halfway to the North Pole (45-degree latitude) and you looked east again for the sunrise. The sun would still rise directly in front of you, but as it rises it will tilt off to your right side and at noon it will not be directly above, but instead off to your right at 45 degrees. The sun will continue to set diagonally in the west.

Knowing the path of the sun throughout the year will help you decide where to aim your solar modules. You should always aim your modules due south if you live in the northern hemisphere (or due north if you live in the southern hemisphere). With off grid solar systems you always want to optimize for the worst-case scenario which is usually in the wintertime. In that case it will benefit you to increase the tilt angle of your modules for a lower sun altitude. If you use most of your energy in the afternoon, aim your modules off to the west. *It is best to produce solar energy closest to the time when you want to use it.*

Solar Window

The solar window frames the extremes of the sun path in your site location. You should aim your modules toward your solar window to maximize energy production. As discussed above regarding the path of the sun, the farther north we are, the more the solar window is pitched to the southern sky. Also, the sun path is a longer line during summer, and shorter in the winter. The most the Sun path will vary between summer and winter is 47 degrees.

Finding True North

In order to effectively locate your solar window, you need to be able to accurately find true north. You could use the stars to help approximate your alignment, but that may not be very precise. You could also use a magnetic compass, but these point to the *magnetic* north, which is slightly off target from the true North Pole.

You can calculate true north by accounting for the **Magnetic Declination** based on your region. In the Americas, the magnetic declination ranges from 20 degrees positive on the west coast to 20 degrees negative on the east coast. Most of Africa and Asia are close to zero and Southern African countries can be as high as 20 degrees negative. Australia is close to zero on the east coast but around 15 degrees positive on the west coast. See the next image to determine the declination for your particular area. The magnetic poles are always fluctuating and they can change in just a few years, so be sure to look up an updated map. Check www.OffGridSolarBook.com for a high resolution image.

2010 WORLD MAGNETIC MODEL FOR DECLINATION

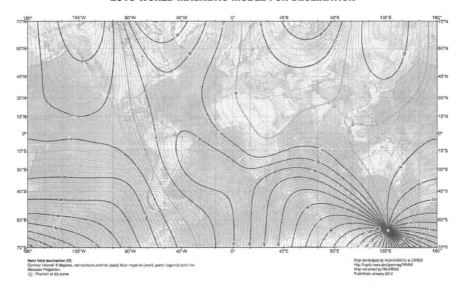

Solar Irradiance (Power)

Solar irradiance is the power from sunlight in a given area and fluctuates depending on site conditions. It is typically expressed in watts per square meter (W/m^2) and the best you can get is about 1000 W/m^2. This is sometimes called peak sun and is a typical solar irradiance at sea level facing directly at the sun on a clear day at noon. Under the right circumstances, this can occasionally get as high as 1250 W/m^2 if your site is high in altitude, there are cloud reflections, or when there are cold but clear winter days.

Solar Insolation (Energy) and Peak Sun Hours

Solar Insolation is essentially the solar irradiance over time. As I mentioned earlier, the sun is not always perfectly aligned with the solar modules, and off-angle sunlight reduces the power output of the system. While the system might reach full solar irradiance in the middle of the day, it will not achieve full power for the *entire* day. Basically, the modules are producing a varying range of power all day long and the power rating specified on the module nameplate is only the maximum.

The solar insolation is often simplified to the equivalent **Peak Sun Hours** (PSH), the equivalent hours of sunlight at 1000 W/m^2. PSH is a figure that can be multiplied by the power rating of the solar modules to match the actual energy production for that day. By simplifying the energy production down to PSH, it is possible to estimate the size requirements of the solar array and the available solar window.

A common pitfall is to overestimate the energy production from your solar system. Even though you have 12+ hours of sunlight between sunrise and sunset, it does not mean you will have 12 PSH or that your 250-watt module will produce a full 250 watts of power throughout the 12-hour day.

The graph below shows how PSH is a simplification of the actual bell curve production. In other words, the area under the bell curve equals that of the area in the rectangle.

EXPLANATION OF PEAK SUN HOURS (PSH)

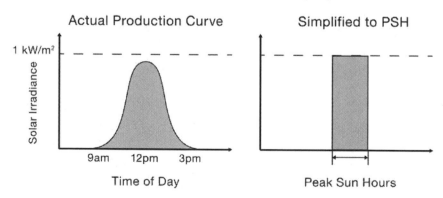

Winter Peak Sun Hours

With off grid systems it is important to design the production of the system to fully recharge the batteries almost every day. Winter production could be as much as 50% lower than summer production. In order to keep the batteries from getting damaged, you must design your solar PV capacity for the worst-case scenario and not the average. Estimating and designing for the worst case solar irradiance during the darkest month in winter will extend the life of your batteries significantly. Winter PSH is a critical metric for an off grid solar energy system.

Designing for winter solar production means that inevitably there will be excess daytime power in the summer months and the batteries will recharge very quickly. Obviously the battery size doesn't change, so the nighttime energy is the same whether it is summer or winter. That said, it's important to consider the extra power available in daytime of the summer months, as it could be used to run additional equipment during those longer summer days. Fans, mills, icemakers, air conditioners, and refrigerators are all good daytime loads to counteract the heat of summer.

Capacity Factor

The Peak Sun Hours (PSH) is a daily average of energy available and helps to determine the efficiency of your energy system. Large power plants typically use the term capacity factor as it represents the efficiency of the power plant. Capacity factor is a ratio of total energy production to the nameplate capacity. It is typically shown as a percentage, but with solar energy systems a common metric is the **Annual Energy Yield**, which is the annual energy production per system size (kWh/kWp). The Annual Energy Yield is a ratio of kilowatt-hours per peak kilowatts (kWh/kWp), and it takes into account all system inefficiencies from the solar cells to the charge controller and inverter. System losses are usually about 15% and an additional 10-20% more if you store all that energy in batteries before using the electricity.

The PSH does not take into account the losses from system inefficiencies. PSH is a useful metric for early stage planning before you design your system, but the Annual Energy Yield is a more realistic metric if you model your production with the actual equipment you plan to use.

If you have limited knowledge about your site location and need to estimate, consider the following: If a system is properly installed with minimal shading and at optimal tilt, you can expect to get between 1200-2000 kWh/kWp annually for a typical fixed-tilt photovoltaic system. In the American southwest, near the Saharan desert, or in the deserts of Australia you can estimate 2000 kWh/kWp, but these locations are exceptionally sunny and few other places will get that much energy. If there are a lot of tall trees around or significant cloud or fog cover most of the year, expect to get less than 1200 kWh/kWp.

GLOBAL SOLAR INSOLATION MAP

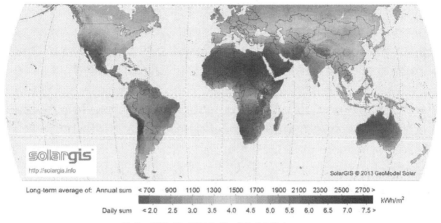

SolarGIS © 2014 GeoModel Solar

The Annual Energy Yield is the energy available before you charge the batteries. If your batteries are fully charged and there is no load on the system, then some of the solar power produced will not get used. This problem is inevitable with off grid solar systems, but with a good load calculation table and load management plan, these losses can be kept to a minimum.

Fixed-Tilt PV Example			
	Insolation Levels		
	Low	Normal	High
Daily Average PSH*	3.5	4.8	6.0
Annual Energy Yield (kWh/kWp)	1200	1550	2000
Capacity Factor	14%	18%	23%

* Before system efficiency losses

Temperature

PV systems are negatively affected by increased heat. In high heat, solar modules are less efficient and batteries can even be damaged. Extremely cold temperatures can actually increase the PV efficiency, but usually have a negative effect on the batteries. Place your batteries indoors away from direct sunlight and preferably in a well-insulated location so that the swings in temperature are kept to a minimum. The PV modules can be passively cooled if they are mounted with space behind them to allow for airflow. It's best to keep a gap of 50 cm or more behind the modules and the mounting surface for optimal heat dissipation. The cell temperature in a solar module is generally 30-40 °C higher than ambient air temperature, and for every degree above 25 °C the module's performance will drop by approximately 0.5%.

Array Design

Now that you understand your site conditions and how to harvest the sunlight for your particular location, you can use this information to design an appropriate system.

Array Orientation

Similar to the two angles used to locate the sun in the sky, there are two angles to define the orientation of the solar array, the **array azimuth** and the **array tilt angle**. The array azimuth tells you if you are aiming the array generally toward the morning sun (east), toward solar noon, or toward the afternoon sun (west). Depending on site conditions and your energy needs, you might prefer a particular array azimuth. For example, if a lot of energy is used in the early afternoon, it might be best to aim the modules toward the west to capture the evening light. This ensures that energy is produced during the times it is being used.

Array Tilt Angle

A good place to start when choosing your array tilt angle is to match your site's latitude angle. For example, in Puerto Rico the latitude is 18 degrees north of the equator, so an array tilt angle of 18 degrees due south would make the solar panels face directly into the sun most of the time.

The array tilt angle is measured from the ground to the back edge of the module. A flat array horizontal to the ground has a tilt angle of zero and is good for systems near the equator. If you're located further north, you will want to increase your array tilt angle toward the southern part of the sky. If you want to optimize for winter, you should increase your array tilt angle by as much as 15 degrees. Note that some solar mounting systems provide adjustability in array tilt so they can be optimized for seasonal changes in sun altitude. See the *System Design* chapter for more details on adjustable tilt racking.

If you plan to mount on your rooftop, it is typically better to mount flush to the roof surface to make installation easier. For flat rooftops, though, it is beneficial to add at least 5 degrees of array tilt. Keep in mind that reducing your tilt angle might make your racking system less expensive or safer in high wind regions. If you are using a pole- or ground-mounted racking system you might be able to design your system for adjustable tilt in order to improve the energy harvest throughout the year.

Design for Your Load Pattern

Equipment operated when the solar panels are producing power is the most efficient use of solar energy. That's because the power does not need to be stored in the batteries. The round-trip efficiency is reduced to 80-95% when stored and used later. With an off grid system, you always want to fully recharge your batteries, but you might also consider adjusting the array tilt and orientation to maximize the solar production when you are using your electricity.

Do you plan to have high loads in the winter? Maybe you want to use an electric hot water heater, which will certainly use more energy in the winter months compared to the summer ones. If this is the case, you should consider increasing your tilt angle to maximize for winter production. Do you plan to use a fan, television, or computer in the afternoon after you get home from work? You might consider aiming your modules to the west to capture the most energy in the afternoon. These are just two examples of how aiming your solar panels can improve your system performance.

Design for a DC or AC System?

Most off grid systems assume that you need AC power, but you should determine beforehand if AC power is actually necessary for you. Charge controllers provide DC power, so the extra cost of using an inverter is only necessary if you plan to use large appliances that require AC power. You could have a simpler system that costs less money and is more efficient if you skip the inverter. Most LED lights and small electronic devices function in DC already and some charge controllers have an output for DC loads. Avoiding the need for inverters and AC power works great for small systems and portable systems where you have complete control over the DC power supplies for the equipment.

If you are dealing with high power or have long wires over 20 meters to connect any of your equipment, then you might consider using an inverter. AC Inverters use a voltage of 120V or 240V whereas DC systems usually are 12V, 24V, or 48V. It's the high voltage, not the fact that it is DC or AC, that is beneficial for the long wire runs. You could also have both a DC and AC load center to access the advantages of each format.

If you choose to design a DC-only system, make sure your appliances are designed for DC use. The Global Off-Grid Lighting Association (GOGLA) published a catalog of DC Appliances called: *Photovoltaics for Productive Use Applications: A Catalogue of DC-Appliances*. It lists DC products that are designed to work directly with DC solar panels or DC batteries, such as water pumps, TVs, radios, communication equipment, freezers, refrigerators, workshop tools, and electric fences as well as equipment for tailoring, hair cutting, food processing, poultry farming, and dairy production.

Design for AC or DC coupled Solar PV?

In some cases, usually for larger solar and battery systems, you can have your solar PV system and your battery system function separately. When AC-coupling a solar and battery system, you use a battery inverter and a PV inverter, then you connect them on their AC circuit. This requires redundant equipment (two inverters) and therefore can cost more money, but it also allows for retrofitting a new battery system with an existing solar PV system.

For off grid systems, there is rarely a good case to have an AC coupled system unless your system is very large or consists of many different systems tied together, which is also called a microgrid. For example, you could have three 8 kW PV systems with simple grid-following inverters and a large 30 kW battery system with a grid-forming inverter. The microgrid is "formed" by the battery inverter and the solar inverters "follow" the microgrid voltage and produce AC power onto the grid.

For the most part, this book is focused on DC-coupled systems, which broadly means the solar PV and batteries are connected on a DC circuit with one inverter. On a DC-coupled system your inverter can be bi-directional (DC-to-AC and AC-to-DC), so it can recharge the batteries from the AC side, typically a grid connection or a generator. But a bi-directional inverter is not necessary and generally costs a lot more than a standard inverter. See the *Inverter Selection* chapter to learn more about bi-directional inverters.

What is a Microgrid?

There are varying definitions of a microgrid, depending on who you ask and the particular context in which the term is used. This section incorporates multiple variations of the term to highlight the key characteristics of a microgrid.

There are grid-tied systems with large energy storage systems and smart electronics that can provide power to an area when the grid fails. In developing countries, there are off grid systems with pay-as-you-go meters. On university campuses, there are combined heat and power systems for groups of buildings.

Technically these are all microgrids, but of different types. The best but most inclusive definition I have seen is from the Microgrid Institute:

A microgrid is a small energy system capable of balancing captive supply and demand resources to maintain stable service within a defined boundary.

Key Characteristics of a Microgrid:

1. Connecting to the traditional grid is *optional.*
2. Resiliency, reliability, and sustainability are the core responsibilities.
3. Backup for all system loads, not just the critical loads.
4. Modern technology is needed to optimize energy production and usage.

According to the US Department of Energy:

A microgrid is a local energy grid with control capability, which means it can disconnect from the traditional grid and operate autonomously.

According to the Rocky Mountain Institute:

Microgrids are subsets of the greater grid and usually include their own generation (such as photovoltaics, wind turbines, and fuel cells), their own demand (lights, fans, televisions, computers, etc.) and often the ability to modulate it to match price and priority, and perhaps even storage capability (such as batteries or the distributed storage in electrified vehicles). What makes the microgrid unique is that it intelligently coordinates and balances all these technologies.

According to the Microgrid Institute:

A microgrid is a small energy system capable of balancing captive supply and demand resources to maintain stable service within a defined boundary. **Microgrids are defined by their function, not their size.** *Microgrids combine various distributed energy resources (DER) to form a whole system that's greater than its parts.*

Most microgrids can be further described by one of five categories (as defined by the Microgrid Institute):

- **Off grid microgrids** including islands, remote sites, and other microgrid systems not connected to a local utility network.
- **Campus microgrids** that are fully interconnected with a local utility grid, but can also maintain some level of service in isolation from the grid, such as during a utility outage. Typical examples serve university and corporate campuses, prisons, and military bases.
- **Community microgrids** that are integrated into utility networks. Such microgrids serve multiple customers or services within a community, generally to provide resilient power for vital community assets.
- **District Energy microgrids** that provide electricity as well as thermal energy for heating (and cooling) of multiple facilities.
- **Nanogrids** comprised of the smallest discrete network units with the capability to operate independently. A nanogrid can be defined as a single building or a single energy domain.

Microgrid Challenges

The main difference between a standard off grid system and a true microgrid, is that a microgrid usually has many end users of electricity. It also might have more than one generation source. These additional complexities require more equipment to measure, divert and disconnect loads.

For example, if a community builds a microgrid with a large solar and battery system, then each home in that community should have a local meter to measure (and sometimes disconnect) the power and energy usage. If each home is expected to pay their portion of the electricity, then the local meter needs to accurately measure the energy used and disconnect if the credits run out. There are many types of payment systems for microgrids, such as pay-as-you-go or prepayment. All require some type of infrastructure for credit card payments, website payments, or even payment via cell phone minutes. Most functioning microgrids I have visited require person-to-person transactions to buy credits, necessitating staff to manage payments.

Microgrids also have a significant electrical load side infrastructure compared to a typical off grid system. This could include substantial wiring from the generation site to multiple end users with sub panels and redundant connections, or even high voltage transformers with overhead cabling for longer distances.

At this point you should have a good understanding of how you will use energy on your site and the general capabilities of your location. Next we will explore the specific technology in more detail, so you can choose the right equipment for the job.

Battery Selection

Now that you understand the load profile for your system and your local solar energy capabilities, you need to choose appropriate equipment for your off grid solar energy system. Before engineering a detailed system, there are a few things to do first. Start by selecting batteries, since they define how long you can provide power without sunshine available. After that, select the type of solar modules, charge controller, inverter, and balance of system components (i.e., all minor electrical and mechanical equipment, discussed later in this book).

Now is a good time for a refresher on voltage, current, and resistance. **Voltage**, the measure of electric potential, is measured in volts (V). Voltage measures the difference in electrical potential between two parts of a circuit and is commonly compared to pressure. For example, imagine two water buckets: one full of water, the other one empty. If a pipe connects the two near the bottom, the water will rush from the full bucket to the empty bucket, because of the water pressure. The same thing will happen if you connect a solar module and a battery. As long as the solar panel has a higher voltage, or "pressure," it will push energy into the battery.

Current, also known as amperage, is the measure of electrical flow and is measured in amperes or amps (A). You can think of this as the number of electrons moving through a conductor in a given time period. One ampere is literally the measurement of 6 billion billion (6.2415×10^{18}) electrons per second!

If a circuit has no voltage, then it has no current. Or in other words, if there is no difference in electric potential, then there will be no flow of electricity.

Electrical **Resistance** is a measure of how much a conductor opposes the passage of electrons. It represents the difficulty of electricity to flow and is measured in Ohms (Ω). Resistance is the ratio of voltage to current, so if you want low resistance then you want high voltage compared to current. See the *Understanding Electricity* chapter at the end of the book for a more detailed description of voltage, current, and resistance.

OK, now back to batteries, the energy containers of your off grid solar system. **Lead-acid** batteries are the most common type, and the majority of this chapter is about them. **Lithium-ion** batteries are popular in small products and electric vehicles (EVs) and are becoming more common in solar energy systems. When the battery system also includes the Battery Management System (BMS), safety equipment, and inverter, it is often referred to as an Energy Storage System (ESS) or Battery Energy Storage System (BESS).

Other Battery Types

There are many battery technologies in the world, each with their own unique benefits and limitations. However, I will only discuss the battery types that are relevant to an off grid solar energy system. Below is a list of less common battery chemistries. Only a few manufacturers support them, but you might find these battery types at a discount and want to use them regardless of other drawbacks.

Sodium-Ion batteries are made from nontoxic materials that are non-flammable. They tend to have a long cycle life and won't be damaged when left in partial charge for long periods of time. They are heavy and large for the amount of energy that they provide, similar in size and weight to lead-acid batteries. Their biggest disadvantage is that they must be charged or discharged slowly due to their high internal resistance.

Nickel-Iron (NiFe) batteries are a very old technology invented by Swedish inventor Waldemar Jungner back in 1899 and commercialized by Thomas Edison in 1901. NiFe Batteries have a very long lifecycle, lasting up to 30 years, and are very tolerant to abuse from overcharging, over-discharging, and short circuiting. The trouble with NiFe batteries is that they are 3-4 times less efficient compared to other battery types. Also, many inverters and charge controls can't handle the large voltage difference between the fully charged and discharged state.

Nickel-Cadmium (NiCd) batteries are rugged and have a relatively high cycle life but they are made with toxic cadmium, which can cause serious problems if not disposed of properly. Recently, NiCd batteries have begun to be replaced by **Nickel-Metal-Hydride (NiMH) batteries,** which are similar to NiCd but with slightly improved performance. NiCd and NiMH batteries are good for extremely low maintenance systems.

Zinc-Air batteries have similarities to fuel cells. When charging a zinc-air battery, the electricity converts the zinc oxide to zinc and oxygen. When zinc is separated away from oxygen there is potential energy available. During the discharging process, the battery combines the zinc and oxygen which generates an electric charge. Zinc batteries have been studied for a very long time, but few companies have found ways to commercialize the battery technology.

To learn more about batteries I recommend reading the content on www.BatteryUniversity.com

Lead-Acid Batteries

There are many trade-offs when selecting a battery and that makes every project different. Common, relatively inexpensive lead-acid batteries can be suitable for most systems. Lithium-ion batteries could be suitable for your system, but as a new technology they might not be as readily available. In the next few years, lithium-based batteries will become more cost effective and will likely replace the less efficient lead-acid technology.

If lead-acid batteries are maintained properly, they will function at 80-90% efficiency. It is important to store a full charge whenever possible, because this will extend battery life and maintain a higher efficiency. Lead-acid batteries can be damaged if overcharged or over-discharged. In this chapter, I will explain how to properly maintain batteries to increase their usable life.

Buy Deep-Cycle Batteries, Not Car Batteries

Batteries designed to start a car engine are NOT recommended for use with a solar PV system. Starter batteries are readily available around the world and relatively inexpensive because of the automobile industry, but they will stop functioning within 3 to 12 months if used with a solar energy system.

For solar charging applications, you want a **Deep-Cycle battery**, similar to those used for boats or electric vehicles — a typical car battery will not work. Sometimes called *motive power* or *traction* batteries, deep-cycle batteries are designed to be deeply discharged regularly using a large portion of their capacity. Deeply discharging a starter battery too frequently harms the thin plates, so deep-cycle batteries are constructed with thicker plates and different chemistry to handle deeper charging cycles.

Starter batteries used in automobiles deliver short, high-current bursts to start an engine and are meant to discharge only a small amount of their capacity. They are also called Starting, Lighting and Ignition (SLI) batteries. Starter batteries are designed to stay nearly 100% fully charged most of the time. The internal architecture of these types of batteries has a large number of thin plates for increased surface area, which provides a quick burst of current when needed. If batteries like these are used for a PV system, they will quickly fail because the internal architecture is not designed for the deep charge and discharge cycles that are common in an off grid PV system.

Lead-Acid Battery Types

Now that you know to look for a Deep-Cycle battery, which one should you choose? It depends on how you plan to maintain your batteries. If you are setting up a remote solar energy system without anyone available to provide maintenance, then you should consider Valve-Regulated Lead-Acid (VRLA) batteries. If you plan on having someone maintain the batteries, and they are able to maintain them about once a month, then you should consider Flooded Lead-

Acid batteries, since they are about half the cost of VRLA batteries.

Lead-acid batteries have large capacities and are available in many places around the world. The flooded type is less common and requires more maintenance compared to other batteries; however, it also tends to provide the lowest cost per kWh.

Sealed or Valve-Regulated Lead-Acid (VRLA)

There are two main types of "sealed" batteries: **Gelled** and **Absorbed Gas Mat (AGM)**. They technically are not sealed but are valve regulated to allow for gasses to escape. If you want a low maintenance system, then a sealed battery may be your best bet. Since VRLA will not spill like flooded batteries can, you can mount them in many positions.

*Remember that all lead-acid batteries require proper ventilation even if they are labeled as "sealed" batteries.

Gel Batteries do perform better than AGM Batteries in high temperatures, but they need to be recharged very slowly, which is not optimal for solar. AGM batteries are typically lighter and less expensive per amp-hour compared to gel. Gel batteries are useful in situations where there is significant vibration, because the gel stops the electrolyte from moving around. There are rarely any vibration or rotation problems with PV installations, so the advantages of gel batteries are not usually applicable.

Flooded Lead-Acid

Flooded batteries are about half the cost of VRLA, are slightly lighter per energy capacity, and tend to come in larger capacities. They require monitoring and measuring at least once every three months. The chances for failure are higher with flooded batteries if they are poorly maintained. Flooded batteries require adequate ventilation and should not be stored in living spaces. They also have the potential problem of tipping over and spilling corrosive acid.

Flooded batteries are a good choice for larger off grid systems when there are over 2,000 watts of PV and someone is able to maintain the equipment on a monthly basis. There is further discussion of necessary maintenance of these batteries in the next section.

Tubular Plate, Flooded Lead-Acid

Flooded lead-acid batteries come in two types: tubular plate and flat plate. The tubular plate is also often called "OPzS", a German acronym that stands for: O = Ortsfest (stationary), Pz = PanZerplatte (tubular plate), and S = Flüssig (flooded). Because of their construction tubular plate batteries have a longer life and provide more cycles compared to other lead-acid technologies. Because of this OPzS can have the lowest cost of ownership because their total energy throughput is significantly larger compared to other lead-acid batteries while the upfront cost is only marginally higher.

They can be shipped "dry" without electrolyte so they last longer in storage and are lighter for shipment. In that case you will need to find sulfuric acid and prepare the right diluted mixture for your local climate. For hotter climates you can use less sulfuric acid and for colder climates you should use more to prevent freezing.

Tubular plate flooded batteries tend to be used for larger capacity projects and are often used for remote telecom projects. They can last as long as 20 years even with a depth of discharge as high as 80%, but if used in hotter climates their cycle life can be radically reduced.

Maintenance for Flooded Lead-Acid Batteries

Specific Gravity

Part of the maintenance required with flooded batteries is measuring the electrolyte fluid inside of the battery and checking for the specific gravity. This tells you about the depth of charge and the status of the battery. Specific gravity is the ratio of the density of the electrolyte solution to the standard density of water. In colder climates, this ratio should be increased to reduce the chance of freezing. Specific gravity can be decreased in areas with hotter weather since battery freezing is not likely and this will prolong the life of the battery. The battery should get an equalized charge if the specific gravity is inconsistent between cells.

Hydrometers measure the specific gravity of a battery's fluid and can then accurately determine its voltage. If the difference in voltage between cells is more than 0.2V, then it is time to equalize. A large difference of voltage between cells is also a sign of a malfunctioning/dead battery or a sign of sulfated cells.

Equalizing

You can extend the life of your flooded lead-acid batteries if an equalizing charge is applied once or twice a month. An **equalizing charge** is a special boosted charge that increases the voltage about 10% higher than usual and is applied for up to 16 hours. Equalizing ensures all the cells in the battery are equally charged and creates gas bubbles that help mix the electrolyte fluid. Always let the batteries sit for at least three hours before you equalize. Follow the instruction on your charge controller or inverter for details on how to apply an equalizing charge.

AGM and gelled batteries can also be equalized a few times a year, but check with the manufacturer before doing so. Note that you should never equalize lithium batteries. For more guidance on maintaining your batteries see the *Operations and Maintenance* chapter.

Lithium-Ion Batteries

For decades lead-acid batteries have been the dominant choice for off grid solar systems, but with the growth of electric vehicles (EVs), lithium-ion (Li-ion) battery technology has improved and become a viable option for off grid solar. Nevertheless, keep in mind that using lithium-ion batteries in your off grid solar system adds another layer of complexity to your system, so be sure you are up for the design challenge.

In 2016, lithium-ion batteries were just beginning to be used for large-scale solar systems, but they have been used for portable and handheld solar systems for years. Due to their enhanced energy density and ease of transport, they are worth serious consideration for portable energy systems.

While Li-ion batteries have their advantages for small, portable solar projects, I would be hesitant to recommend them for all larger systems. Most of the off grid charge controllers and inverters on the market today are designed for lead-acid batteries, meaning the built-in set points for protection devices are not designed for lithium-ion batteries. Using these electronics with a lithium-ion battery would result in communication problems with the Battery Management System (BMS) protecting the battery. That being said, there are already some manufacturers that sell charge controllers for Li-ion batteries and that number is likely to grow in the future.

The graph below illustrates how lithium-ion batteries have generally three times the capacity for the same weight and twice the capacity for the same volume compared to lead-acid (flooded, AGM, and gel). Lithium-ion batteries are in a league of their own when compared to all other battery types since they are significantly more energy dense.

BATTERY DENSITY COMPARISON

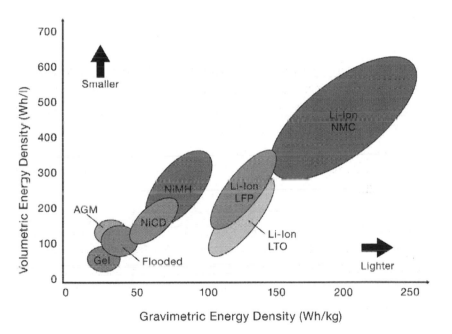

Compared to lead-acid batteries, lithium-ions are also more resilient to damage from deep discharging, do not need to be brought to a full state of charge each cycle, function better in hot climates, and last up to three times longer.

There are many types of lithium-ion batteries, but the three most common and relevant to solar are:

- **LFP**: Lithium Iron Phosphate
  - o Typically has the highest cycle life
  - o Lowest energy density of the lithium batteries due to its lower operating voltage
  - o Sometimes also includes manganese to increase performance
- **LTO**: Lithium Titanate
  - o Can be discharged a very high rates
  - o Cycle count is said to be higher than other Li-ion
  - o Functions better at low-temperature
  - o Typically expensive and low energy density
- **NMC**: Lithium Nickel Manganese Cobalt Oxide
  - o The preferred chemistry for EVs because of the high energy density
  - o There are many combinations such as 811 and 111, which are just the ratios of each of the three materials. (For example, NMC-811 is 80% N, 10% M, and 10% C)
  - o Typically high power for discharge and low internal resistance
  - o Good cycle life, but not as good as LFP
- **NCA**: Lithium Nickel Cobalt Aluminum Oxide
  - o Also popular in EVs
  - o Lowest performance on cycle life of the three on this list

Cobalt Problems

Cobalt is a rare earth metal that is only found in large supplies in a few locations around the world, such as China, Zambia, Russia and Australia, and a major mining industry is in one of Africa's most unstable regions, the Democratic Republic of the

Congo. (Ironically, this is not too far from where I installed solar microgrids with batteries containing cobalt.)

Historically, the brutal working conditions in small-scale cobalt mines and refineries have been disregarded in order to meet the rising market demand driven by the automotive industry. But many global automotive companies are realizing that they may not want to participate in cobalt mines with unsafe working conditions and child labor. In 2017, an organization called First Cobalt adopted the Responsible Cobalt Initiative (RCI) as part of a collective response to these concerns. The goal of RCI is to improve these conditions in the mines, but it might also divert profits away from small scale miners.

Many solar and battery companies who want to avoid these conflict minerals are simply choosing LFP type batteries since these contain no conflict minerals like cobalt.

In addition to the problems of sourcing Cobalt, independent scientific studies have shown that LFP batteries have a better thermal stability than NMC batteries. Precisely, LFP exhibited a better response to each of the following critical failure mode: (i) short-circuit; (ii) overdischarge; and (iii) overcharge. These results have been explained by the difference in chemical structure, as LFP's olivine structure is able to trap oxygen atoms and prevent exothermal decomposition reactions. The National Fire Protection Association (NFPA) concluded in a recent report that "all stages of testing showed the LFP modules presented a lower fire hazard risk than the NMC."

Given the option to choose, it's hard not to see that LFP is the best option for solar and battery energy storage systems. If a battery company is using NMC or NCA, it's probably because they are repurposing batteries from another application such as electric vehicles. NMC and NCA are the highest in energy density so there can be some advantages over LFP if there are space or weight constraints.

Lithium-Ion Lifecycle

The internal chemistry of Li-ion batteries allows them to last longer than lead-acid in almost all scenarios. For example, if you discharged to 50% then recharged to 100% every day, then a lithium-ion battery would last at least three times longer than a lead-acid battery with the same capacity.

Most Li-ion batteries can be discharged up to 80% without significant damage to the battery's capacity, while lead-acid generally shouldn't be discharged beyond 50% of capacity. Because of the significant difference in depth of discharge and total lifecycle, it is not entirely fair or accurate to simply compare the initial cost and capacity of the two battery types when calculating total value.

Unlike lead-acid, lithium-ion batteries do not experience a sudden death failure, but rather have a continual decrease in capacity and increased internal resistance.

Safety Issues

Thermal runaway occurs when the cell rapidly heats and can release electrolyte, flames, and dangerous fumes. Both lead-acid and lithium-ion batteries are capable of overheating and going into thermal runaway, but it is more common with lithium-ion because these have more energy packed into a smaller volume. Specifically, the cobalt in NMC and NCA types is particularly flammable and does not self-extinguish. Of all the lithium-based batteries, LFPs, which contain no cobalt, are least likely to have thermal runaway problems.

Independent scientific studies have shown that LFP Li-Ion batteries have a better thermal stability than NMC Li-Ion batteries. LFP exhibited a better response to the following critical failure mode: short-circuit, over discharge, and overcharge. The National Fire Protection Association (NFPA) concluded that all stages of testing showed the LFP modules presented a lower fire hazard risk than the NMC.

Most lithium-ion batteries come equipped with a Battery Management System (BMS) or some kind of protective equipment integrated into the battery to protect it from a thermal runaway event. The BMS will disconnect the load on the battery any time it senses a potential problem from temperature, current surges, or voltage variations. That is why it is critical to ALWAYS use a BMS or other protective circuit with any lithium battery.

Battery Management System (BMS)

Lithium-ion batteries always require some electronics to protect the cells from extreme voltage, current, or temperatures In many cases, a proprietary **Battery Management System (BMS)** comes with a battery pack to equalize and protect the individual battery cells. But you can also build a battery pack by assembling cells and adding a BMS. Most batteries other than lithium-ion do not require a BMS for safe usage. Lithium batteries are unique in this way because they can easily catch on fire if the voltage, peak current, or temperature for an individual cell is not kept under control.

A BMS monitors each cell and will only function if each cell remains in a safe voltage range. Some mistakenly think they can ensure safety by simply keeping the overall pack voltage below a safe limit, ignoring the individual cell voltage. The problem with this approach is that it assumes that all the cells are in exact balance. In reality all battery cells have unique variations and they rarely maintain the same voltage due to internal characteristics. This causes cells to capture and release varying amounts of energy; in other words, cells drift on their state of charge and specific voltage. Because of this, when a battery pack is charged and discharged many times, the cells can become out of balance.

For example, if a pack voltage is measured at 28.8V for 8 cells in series, you might think that all cells are at 3.6V by taking the average of the pack voltage per cell.

$$28.8V / 8 \text{ cells} = 3.6 \text{ average V per cell}$$

If the cells are in perfect balance, then each cell would be at 3.6V. But all cells do not function the same. Every battery cell (lithium, lead-acid, etc.) is a unique snowflake. Its capacity, impedance characteristics, and aging patterns are all slightly different.

The magic of a BMS is that it can help you with these variations between cells. It can actively rebalance or discharge the highest cells so the average cell voltage and each individual cell's voltages are close. It can also disconnect the pack if any one cell gets into an unsafe condition.

In the example above with a pack voltage of 28.8V, without a BMS there is no way to tell if any one cell has reached its maximum voltage limit. Below is an example of two packs with the same pack voltage but with very different cell voltages. Without a BMS there is no way to stop Cell #5 from overcharging.

EXAMPLE OF TWO DIFFERENT PACKS WITH THE SAME PACK VOLTAGE

	Out of Balance Pack (V)	Perfectly Balanced Pack (V)
Cell 1	3.60	3.60
Cell 2	3.53	3.60
Cell 3	3.57	3.60
Cell 4	3.50	3.60
Cell 5	**4.03**	3.60
Cell 6	3.49	3.60
Cell 7	3.54	3.60
Cell 8	3.54	3.60
Pack Voltage	28.80	28.80

Some recommend managing the peak voltage on a cell by "top balancing" each cell before assembling the pack. This refers to manually charging all cells up to a peak voltage so that they all match. After they "top balance" the cells, they only monitor the pack voltage. They fail to consider that over time, all cells will naturally drift from each other and cell voltages will eventually not match at the top of the charge. It is possible to always monitor and manually balance the cells in a pack, but with one mistake or forgetting to check often enough, there could be disastrous consequences. It is best to leave this mundane task to the BMS. As I described above, measuring exclusively pack voltage is a dangerous practice, as top balancing only *reduces* but does not eliminate the chance of thermal runaway.

Functions of a BMS

A BMS has sensors for voltage, current, and temperature to measure many battery parameters to determine the State of

Charge (SOC) and the State of Health (SOH). It will measure
and sometimes record the following:

- **Voltage**: Voltage per cell, maximum and minimum,
  and pack voltage
- **Current**: Amperage going in and out of the battery,
  peak current, and maximum pulse current
- **Temperature**: at least one temperature sensor near the
  part of the battery that gets the hottest

The Depth of Discharge (DOD) is the percentage of energy
used compared to its original capacity and is the reverse of the
State of Charge. The **State of Charge (SOC)** is the estimated
percent of energy currently available in the battery, similar to
a gas tank gauge in a car. A 10% SOC is the same as 90%
DOD. A BMS will measure the voltage for each cell and also
measure the current flowing in and out of the battery. It will
run a calculation to estimate the SOC. Because this is only an
estimation, the BMS may recalculate ("jump") to a
substantially different SOC level depending on the data
flowing in.

State of Health (SOH) is the ratio of the current capacity of
the battery as it compares to its original capacity. A 100% SOH
means the battery is functioning like new, whereas at 70-80%
SOH, manufacturers typically recommend retiring and
replacing it. Battery capacity generally decreases in a linear
fashion with use and time, so after a few years of typical usage
you can predict when it will be time to replace your batteries
based on the SOH. The SOH for most batteries drops linearly
during the middle of their designed life then can drop
dramatically and quickly. Some Lithium-ion cells will start to
drop as early as 500 cycles, but typically they last at least 2,000
cycles before this happens, while other Lithium-ion
chemistries won't drop dramatically until 10,000 cycles. It can
be challenging to estimate when this drop off will happen,
because it depends on so many variables. I recommend being

wary of what battery manufacturers advertise and consider the nameplate description as the best case scenario. Review warranty details as this is a better method to estimate the life of the battery.

System Communication

Before purchasing any battery equipment, confirm that the manufacturer has approved its compatibility with other components of your system. Many BMSs require a wake signal in order to operate the battery, so ensure that your BMS or battery is capable of operating and interfacing with the other components. Communication between the BMS and other equipment, such as a charge controller or inverter, can be challenging, since many manufacturers haven't taken the time to test their equipment with all others', nor have they created a common communication platform. CANBUS and MODBUS are communication languages used by a lot of power equipment, but the same language doesn't itself ensure that two devices can actually talk to one another. It is possible to create your own interface that can ping all of your equipment and pull data, but that requires writing code.

If you choose to use a lithium-ion battery, ensure that the charge controller has a communication line that can trigger the BMS to reconnect with the battery after a disconnection event occurs. For example, should the SOC drop below a certain threshold, the BMS will disconnect from the load to protect the battery. This could confuse the charge controller into thinking the battery has been removed from the system or a fuse has been blown, meaning it would no longer send any solar power to recharge battery.

PCM/PCB (Protection Circuit Module or Board)

A simpler version of a BMS would be a PCM or PCB (Protection Circuit Module or Board). A PCM is an analog device that does not store or provide any data. Its sole purpose is to protect the battery cells without any information about the system. These can be significantly cheaper and are often integrated into lithium batteries. If high/low voltage, high/low current, or high/low temperatures are detected the PCM/PCB will disconnect the battery from the load. If you have a PCM/PCB then a BMS is not required.

The biggest disadvantage with PCMs is that you cannot accurately determine the SOC. Also, if the PCM determines an unsafe condition it will disconnect without giving you any indication of why. Most PCMs are inexpensive and commonly poor quality. They are very easy to break during assembly because the electronics are so sensitive. Using a PCM can be a cost-effective solution, but keep these disadvantages in mind when building your battery system. If you decide to build a pack with a PCM, expect to break a few of them, and buy some extras for back ups.

BMS Components

A BMS or PCM must be able to disconnect the battery during a potentially unsafe event, such as a short circuit. It may use an electrically controlled switch to disconnect the battery from the system if it detects a condition that is unsafe. This collection of components that accompany the BMS can consist of Contactors, Relays, fuses, shunts, busbars, and connectors.

Contactors, Relays, and FETs are the electrically controlled switches that BMS and PCM devices use to disconnect the circuit. A **Contactor** is usually used when disconnecting a circuit over 100A, but for lower currents, Relays and FETs can be used. **Relays** are basically smaller Contactors and function in a very similar way. **FETs** (Field Effect Transistors) such as **MOSFETs** are components on a circuit board that also have some inherent resistance, so with high current they can create a lot of heat and energy loss. Contactors and Relays are generally safer than FETs in their failure modes, so often FETs are used as the signal circuit to control the Contactors or Relays. These examples above all have two circuit connections, a low voltage circuit that serves as a signaling channel that the BMS or PCM uses to keep the disconnect open or closed, and a high power circuit that serves as the main high power switch.

BASIC DIAGRAM OF A RELAY

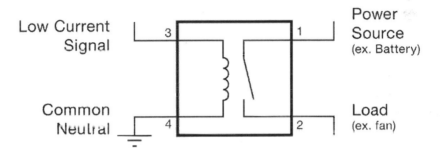

These devices should not be disconnected while under a large load, otherwise they might malfunction. Ideally the charge controller would decrease the load before they disconnected from the system. However, it is possible to disconnect a high power connection that is under load if the charge controller is not responding properly. But there is a danger that the switch that is meant to disconnect the battery may fuse the disconnecting surfaces when the switch is pulling away from the connection. As you can imagine when a lot of power is flowing through a circuit and the switch is then physically disconnected, the two surfaces, just nanometers apart, may still have electrons jump between them. This can cause the two surfaces to weld together (this is exactly how a welding machine functions). It is important to use a suitable disconnect that is rated for the worst case current of your system; an additional fuse can be used to interrupt short circuit current

When a BMS measures the state of charge (SOC) it can measure the cell voltages and pack voltages, but this can be a misleading reading since the voltage can change significantly when under load. A better way to measure the SOC in a battery is to measure the current flow into or out of the battery and compare that to its capacity. There are two devices that can measure current: a Shunt and a Current Transducer.

A **Shunt** is calibrated to allow current to flow through a predefined resistance, and a BMS can measure each side of the shunt to determine current flow in both directions using Ohm's Law. A **Current Transducer**, commonly called a **CT**, measures the magnetic field around the battery wire to estimate the current flowing in and out of the battery. The CT is a sensor shaped like a ring that clips around the battery wire; it does not interrupt the circuit since it indirectly measures the current flow. A CT is not as accurate as a Shunt, but is often less expensive and easier to install. Because a Shunt is built to have the battery current flowing through it, it can more accurately measure the current compared to a CT, which leads to a more accurate SOC value. A BMS will specify what current measuring device is required, because these devices need to be properly calibrated to be effective. Both devices require software calculations that can only be done with a BMS or the more advanced PCMs. The less expensive PCMs without software cannot measure current flow and can only use voltage to determine the SOC.

In some energy storage systems the inverter and power electronics have a large bank of capacitors that are used to filter or buffer the current flow through the system. Suddenly filling up all those capacitors when the system is first turned on and the batteries are connected can result in a damaging amount of current surging through the battery. This can happen in nanoseconds and a human cannot perceive this process. This sudden surge of power acts like a short circuit on the batteries and the BMS might disconnect the battery as a safety mechanism or the fuse might blow. In order to avoid this sudden surge, a **Pre-charge Circuit** can be used to provide some resistance so the capacitors charge slower without causing any problems for the battery. It is important to use the correctly sized resistor that will match the capacitance of the attached equipment. Talk to your BMS provider to determine if the pre-charge resistor is appropriate for your system.

A Pre-charge Circuit could be in the battery pack or the inverter. It consists of a resistor and a switch, such as a Contactor, Relay or FET and is a parallel path to the main connection. The Pre-charge Circuit will connect when the main switch is disconnected and then it will disconnect after the main switch connects. This can all happen in less than a second and must be controlled by the BMS or inverter. See the example in the figure below.

EXAMPLE OF PRE-CHARGE CIRCUIT

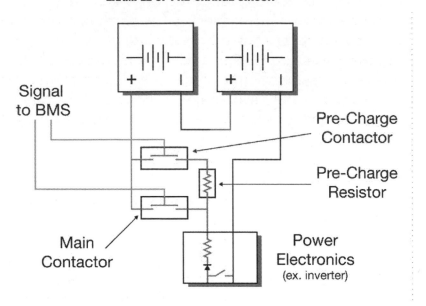

Second Life (Recycled) Batteries

Building a battery from used cells requires a strong foundation in battery and electrical knowledge and I only recommend it for experts. I have seen a lot of people on the internet repurposing old laptop batteries and batteries from electric vehicles. This is a great way to acquire low cost, high quality batteries, but it does require a lot of work to disassemble, test, and sort them. I think this will become a common method in the future because a battery that doesn't work well for an electric vehicle might still be a good fit for a battery energy storage system (BESS), since the charge and discharge rates are so much lower in a BESS compared to an EV. Typically a BESS uses much lower power compared to an EV that needs to accelerate quickly. When building a recycled battery pack, make sure the capacity is large enough that it takes many hours to discharge; ideally it would take two to four hours to discharge even at full power.

When batteries age, their internal resistance increases, which means the effective available energy will decrease over time. This is because when under load, a higher resistance will result in a more significant voltage drop. If the voltage drops too low, then the system loses power. You can imagine this like a clogged pipe where the narrowing pipe allows less flow than before when the pipe was not clogged.

Building a lithium battery pack from used cells is a great way to save money and get more life out of something that would otherwise be discarded. Do not underestimate how useful a BMS can be to monitor and protect you from an unsafe condition, especially when using recycled cells. Please note that since a BMS set up incorrectly will not protect your pack from thermal runaway, you need to contact an expert to ensure the BMS is properly configured to protect the specific cells you are using. Once you build your system you should test to see if your BMS functions as you configured it. For example, you could get a variable DC power supply and simulate a high voltage event and see if the BMS actually disconnects the pack terminals. You could also blow hot air over the temperature sensors to see if a high temperature event will cause the BMS to disconnect the pack terminals.

As I mentioned earlier, every battery cell is as unique as a snowflake, with microscopic variations on the cathode and anode material that result in slight functional variations. When manufacturers build new packs they grade and sort cells so that packs have nearly identical characteristics. They consider energy capacity, internal impedance, and manufacturing date. When you are building your pack from used cells, I recommend you do the same. If you want to build a 16 cell pack, you should buy more than 16 cells and "cherry pick" the best to match. If you use a high quality BMS, you can manage the variations and rebalance the pack after each cycle.

Battery Type Considerations

Flooded Lead-Acid vs. VRLA vs. Lithium-Ion

The initial cost of lithium-ion batteries is significantly higher than lead-acid batteries, but the total lifecycle cost is comparable to and sometimes better than flooded lead-acid. See graphs below.

INITIAL COST PER BATTERY CAPACITY

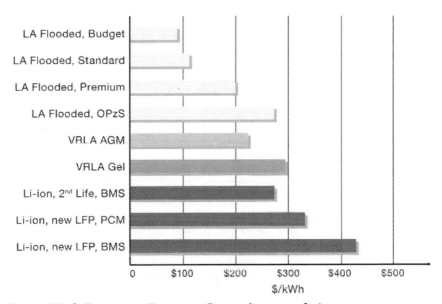

The **Initial Cost per Battery Capacity** graph incorporates:
- The initial cost of the battery
- The full capacity at 20-hour rating
- Note:
  - The Li-ion pack includes BMS or PCM and other equipment so it can be compared fairly to lead-acid batteries
  - Li-ion 2nd Life assumes using old EV batteries

TOTAL LIFECYCLE COST

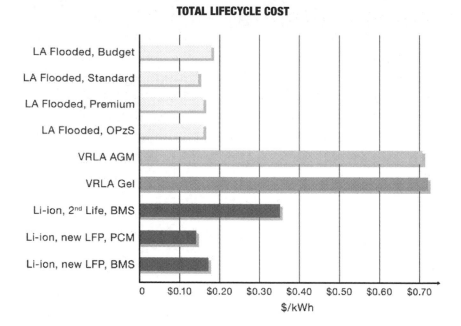

The **Total Lifecycle Cost** graph incorporates the details in the above graph but also includes:

- The representative depth of discharge (DOD) based on the given cycle count
- The round-trip efficiency during a cycle
- The number of cycles until it reaches the standard end of life limit of 80% State of Health (SOH)
  - For the Li-ion, 2nd Life, 1,000 cycles were assumed until the battery was retired

All the data used for the two graphs above utilized the actual details from the representative datasheets and market value. I choose to not list actual manufacturers and instead use an average product from each category.

Depending on which graph you look at first, you can draw drastically different conclusions about which battery technology is most cost effective. The *initial* cost of a battery is important when budgeting for the system, but it can be shortsighted to only focus on keeping the initial cost down when the more expensive battery can save money (or trouble) in the long run.

Flooded batteries have the lowest lifecycle cost but that is assuming they are properly maintained and are not abused. This is assuming the best-case scenario. If they get discharged past 50% frequently or if maintenance is neglected, then they won't last as long, increasing their lifecycle cost. So if low maintenance is important, sealed lead-acid or lithium-ion batteries would be more desirable. When considering all the factors above, lithium-ion batteries become more appealing for an off grid solar energy system.

When comparing lead-acid to lithium-ion batteries, consider the replacement cost of the lead-acid batteries and how to recycle them properly. In a remote location, it could be cost prohibitive to replace the lead-acid batteries every 3-4 years. Also, lead-acid batteries can be recycled, but in some locations, it might be very difficult to dispose of them properly.

FLOODED LEAD-ACID VS. VRLA VS. LITHIUM-ION

	Flooded Lead-Acid	VRLA AGM	Lithium-Ion
Initial Cost per Capacity ($/kWh)	85 - 280	200-240	300 - 1000
Cost per Life Cycle ($/kWh)	$0.17 – 0.25	$0.65 – 0.75	$0.15 – 0.35
Energy Density (Wh/kg)	30	40	120 - 150
Regular Maintenance	Yes	No	No
Number of Cycles to 80% DOD	200 – 2500	200 – 650	1000 – 4000
Typical Depth of Discharge (DOD)	50%	50%	80%
High Temperature Sensitivity	Degrades above 25°C	Degrades above 25°C	Degrades above 45°C
Available Power Constant Current	0.2C	0.3C	1C
Fast Charging Time (hours)	8 – 16	4 – 8	1 – 4

The above information is compiled from my research of specific battery manufacturers and from the Battery University.

Series vs. Parallel Connections

When connecting multiple batteries, you have two options: connect them in series or in parallel. The same goes for connecting many solar modules. You can get double the power when connecting two batteries together, but what about the voltage and the current? What is the voltage and what is the current of two batteries connected together?

Typically Li-ion batteries already come in a package at the desired voltage, so you will only connect them in parallel. However, lead-acid batteries are designed to be connected in series and parallel, so the system can be designed to your specifications.

When you connect the positive lead of one battery to the negative lead of another battery, you are connecting them in **series**. *Series connections double the voltage, but the amperage stays the same.* Alternatively, when you connect batteries in **parallel** you are connecting both of the positive leads and the negative leads together. *Parallel connections double the amperage, but the voltage stays the same.* Note that parallel connections require a parallel connection device such as a multiple input connection terminal, a combiner box, or Y-combiners. Series connections are usually a male-to-female connection and do not need any connection terminals.

The example on the next page shows two batteries and one charge controller. If you connect them in series you get double the voltage, but if you connect them in parallel you get double the amperage. Either way you still end up with 1200 watt-hours.

SERIES VS. PARALLEL BATTERY CONNECTION METHOD

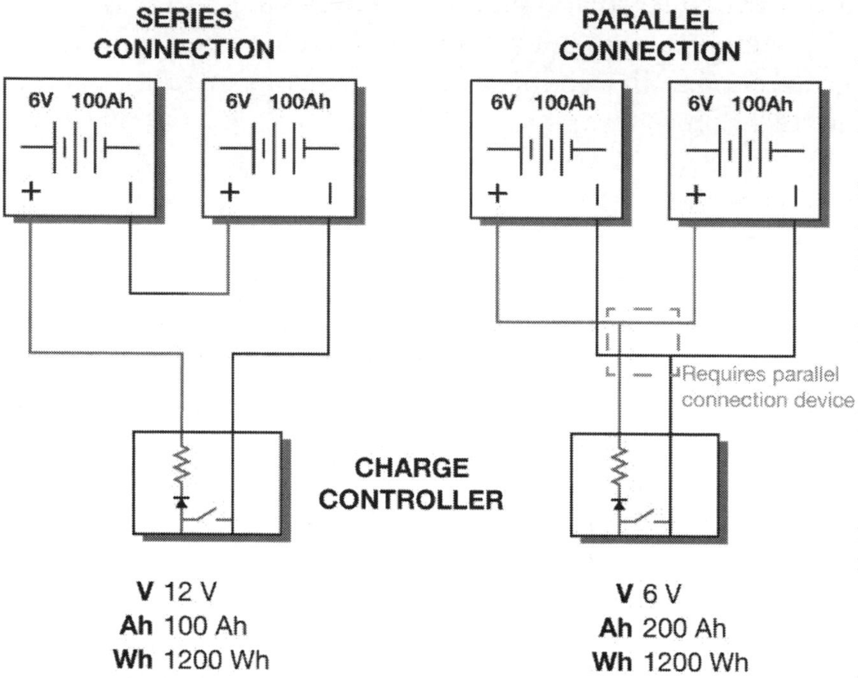

SERIES CONNECTION

PARALLEL CONNECTION

6V 100Ah 6V 100Ah   6V 100Ah 6V 100Ah

CHARGE CONTROLLER

Requires parallel connection device

V 12 V
Ah 100 Ah
Wh 1200 Wh

V 6 V
Ah 200 Ah
Wh 1200 Wh

Connecting low-voltage batteries in series to add up to the desired system voltage is typically better than connecting high voltage batteries in parallel to match the system voltage. The number of strings of lead-acid batteries connected in parallel should be kept to a minimum and rarely exceed 3 parallel connections. This prevents uneven charging between strings of batteries and will put less stress on the batteries. Lithium-ion batteries typically have a BMS allowing for many batteries to be wired in parallel.

Battery Mismatch

Connecting mismatching batteries can be very dangerous and could start a fire.

It is important to allow all the batteries in the same circuit to charge and discharge equally. In order to avoid a potential mismatch that could create an unequal charge, it is recommended to always use batteries of the same age, same manufacturer and model, and same temperature. You should also use larger capacity (and thus lower voltage) batteries to increase system size.

Since wires often have subtle differences that may create a buildup of unequal charges, batteries in parallel must have the same conductor length, wire gauge, and wire type. If batteries are connected in series, a mismatch will not happen because voltage increases and battery capacity stay the same per battery.

Battery Lifespan

There are a variety of factors that will reduce the expected lifespan of a battery and each battery type has its own weaknesses. In the next few sections I will discuss **Depth of Discharge, Rate of Discharge,** and **State of Charge**. The first step is to know what will harm the batteries. Most lead-acid batteries, for example, get damaged if they are discharged below 40% of their State of Charge. When I describe a battery getting "damaged," I am specifically describing a decrease in the battery's State of Health (SOH), which just means the total capacity of the battery has decreased. A 100% SOH means the battery is functioning in a full SOH as the manufacturer intended and an 80% SOH is when manufacturers typically recommend retiring a battery, even though you can continue using them a bit longer.

A helpful way to think of charging and discharging a battery is to imagine it like a balloon. If you repeatedly inflate a balloon to its maximum capacity and then completely deflate it, the balloon material might fatigue from the excessive stress. Now imagine with another balloon you repeatedly inflate and deflate it from 50% to 90% full, the material will experience less stress and will last longer than the first balloon. The plates inside the battery undergo a comparable stress as the balloon material. In this example, lithium-ion batteries are simply made from a better, stronger balloon material when compared to lead-acid.

When you purchase new lead-acid batteries, buy them just before you install them or make sure they don't sit longer than a few months without a full charge. If you buy them early, make sure you never let them get too hot. It is recommended to trickle charge lead-acid batteries before you put them in use. Also note that some brand new lead-acid batteries will not reach their full capacity until they have cycled up to 30 times. During the first few weeks, a battery will likely function 5% to 10% less than its rated capacity.

Below is a table showing the range of time expected for batteries used for an off grid PV system. It is listed as a range because there are many variables that will affect the lifespan, such as the rate and depth of the charge and recharge cycles. Use this table as a general guide, as there is a wide range of lifespan depending on how the battery is used. I will explain why there is such a large fluctuation in lifespan in the next few sections.

EXPECTED LIFESPAN PER BATTERY TYPE

Category	Type	Lifespan
Lead-Acid (Sealed)	Starter (Car battery)	3-12 months
	Gelled Deep-Cycle	2-5 years
	AGM Deep-Cycle	2-8 years
Lead-Acid (Flooded)	Low Quality Deep-Cycle	2-7 years
	Premium Deep-Cycle	7-15 years
	Tubular Plate Deep-Cycle	10-20 years
Other	NiCd (Nickel–Cadmium)	1-20 years
	Li-ion (Lithium-Ion)	5-15 years
	NiFe (Nickel-Iron)	5-35 years

Negative Effects of Extreme Temperatures

In hot temperatures, lithium-ion batteries tend to work better than lead-acid ones. In hot climates, where the average temperature frequently reaches 30 °C or more, the lifecycle for lead-acid batteries drops by approximately 50% compared to its lifecycle at 22 °C rating. Li-ion, however, does not de-rate until temperatures exceed 45 °C.

In very cold climates the electrolyte in lead-acid batteries is more likely to freeze the deeper it is discharged but will function properly if the discharge is kept to a minimum. Below freezing temperatures of 0 °C, Li-ion batteries can be charged very slowly but should be able to discharge.

The graph below shows an example of how the different battery types will function in high and low temperatures. In the "Peak" performance range you can expect the battery to function as described in the datasheet; in the "Low" performance range the battery will function but at a reduced efficiency from "Peak". It is recommended to never use your battery in the "Out of Specification" range, particularly in the high temperature range as this dangerously approaches thermal runaway temperatures. This is just an example; always follow the requirements of the battery's datasheet.

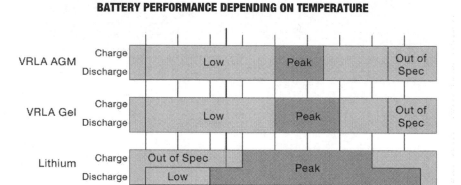

Relationship Between Rate of Discharge and Depth of Discharge

The rate (or speed) at which you charge or discharge a battery is related to the capacity. The faster a battery is discharged, the lower its usable capacity. This is called the **Peukert Effect**, in which the internal resistance of the battery increases as you discharge faster.

The extent of the Peukert Effect is different for each battery type but will increase with any battery's age. Flooded lead-acid batteries tend to have more internal resistance compared to sealed lead-acid, while lithium-ion batteries have low internal resistance until they get old. Below is a table showing the change in capacity when measured at a 20-hour and an 8-hour discharge for different battery chemistries.

**PERCENT REDUCTION IN CAPACITY FROM
20-HR TO 8-HR RATE**

Battery Type	
Lead-Acid (Flooded, Flat)	18%
Lead-Acid (Flooded, Tubular)	14%
Lead-Acid (Sealed AGM)	7%
Lead-Acid (Sealed Gel)	9%
Lithium-Ion	< 1%
Sodium-Ion	31%
Nickel-Iron	10%

Because the capacity of the same lead-acid battery could vary by as much as 35%, the rate at which you discharge or charge is an important consideration when comparing lead-acid batteries. When looking at the capacity, be sure to compare them at the same rate of discharge.

You may notice battery specification sheets have listings of different capacities for the same battery, or you might notice a capacity listed along with a number of hours (something like 250 AH at 100-hour rate). Usually the battery manufacturers list the timeframe in which it is discharged. Always compare batteries at the same discharge rate, so one doesn't appear better than it really is.

Below is a table of the details from a battery specification sheet with their amp-hour value at different rates:

AMP-HOUR CAPACITIES FROM EXISTING PRODUCTS

Battery Category	Battery Type	Amp-Hour Capacity		
		100-hr Rate	20-hr Rate	8-hr Rate
Lead-Acid (Flooded, Plate)	Trojan 6V T-105	250	225	200
	US Battery 6V 2200 XC2	280	232	196
	Surrette 6V S-460 (L-16)	466	350	280
Lead-Acid (Flooded, Tubular)	Victron OPzS Solar 910	901	701	602
Lead-Acid (Sealed AGM)	Concorde 6V PVX-3050T	355	300	280
Lead-Acid (Sealed Gel)	MK 6V 8GGC2 GEL	198	180	165

Depth of Discharge

The lifespan of lead-acid batteries is greatly affected by the depth of discharge; i.e., how much of the battery capacity is used on a daily basis. For example, if a fully charged battery discharges half of its rated capacity, it would be at 50% depth of charge. If the depth of discharge is kept to a minimum, the battery will be capable of more charge/discharge cycles.

The graph on the next page shows the inverse relationship between life cycle and depth of discharge and illustrates how the expected average cycles decrease exponentially as the depths of discharge increase. A general guideline is to design your lead-acid battery systems to have a 50% depth of charge with an absolute maximum of 80% in worst-case scenarios. In very cold climates, this is even more important since the deeper the discharge, the more likely a battery is to freeze. Li-ion batteries are negatively affected by extreme depth of discharge as well, but the effects are less damaging to the long-term health of the battery compared with their lead-acid counterparts.

DOD VS. LIFECYCLE FOR A LEAD-ACID BATTERY

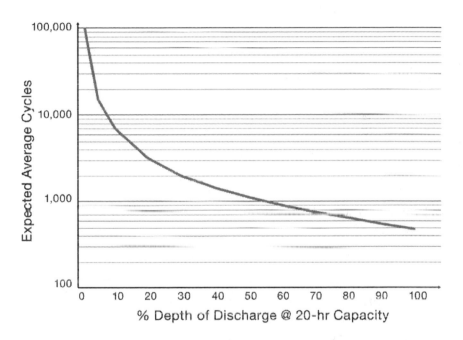

Rate of Charge/Discharge

Sometimes the hour rate of a battery is described as the charge rate (C or C-rate). The **C-rate** relates to how quickly or slowly the battery is charged or discharged relative to its maximum capacity. Rapidly charging or discharging a battery can harm the battery or create unsafe conditions in the rest of the energy system.

C-Rate	Time
5C	12 min
3C	20 min
1C	1 hour
C/2	2 hours
C/5	5 hours
C/8	8 hours
C/10	10 hours

A rate of 1C means a battery will completely discharge in one hour. Therefore, a battery with a rated capacity of 10 Amp-hours at 1C discharges 10 Amps per hour. A 3C rate would discharge the same battery at 30 Amps for slightly less than 20 minutes. Additionally, a C/2 rate would discharge at 5 Amps for slightly more than 2 hours. The C-rate can be written as a fraction or a decimal, for example C/2 is the same as 0.5C.

For Flooded Lead-Acid batteries the fastest charge rate typically should be C/8 for any long periods of time, so for a 100Ah battery you would want to design your system to charge or discharge at no more than 12.5A. If you charge or discharge any faster than that the battery may overheat, lose some of its liquid, or start bubbling. Some manufacturers allow a higher maximum charge rate of about C/3, but these batteries are still susceptible to damage and will need more maintenance and oversight.

State of Charge

The **State of Charge** (SOC) is a measurement of the available capacity of the battery compared to its full capacity and is expressed as a percentage similar the fuel gauge in a car. Unlike a car's fuel tank you do not want to get close to empty, particularly with lead-acid batteries.

Measuring the SOC accurately can be a bit of a challenge. The best way to check the SOC is to use an amp-hour meter or energy meter that measures the current going in or out of the battery. You can also measure the voltage or the specific gravity to approximate the state of charge, but both of those methods can be inaccurate. Checking the specific gravity is only possible for flooded batteries, and it is somewhat inconvenient since you need to open and remove some of the fluid from each cell of each battery. The voltage on a battery will drop when there is a load on it, so to measure the SOC the battery must have no load for at least 6 hours to get an accurate measurement from a multimeter.

Below is a table showing an example of the state of charge with four zones for flooded lead-acid batteries. It is best to stay in the Good Zone and rarely dip into the Unsafe Zone. At minimum, a lead-acid battery should reach 100% SOC every four days to extend its life. If the battery is discharged to less than 40% too often, it will significantly reduce the lifespan.

For example, a 12V nominal flooded lead-acid battery will read 12.7V at 100% charge, 12.0V at 50% charge, and 10.5V at 0% charge. This is the range the battery can function, but you should only let the voltage drop below 2VPC on rare occasions if you want to extend its life.

EXAMPLE FLOODED LEAD-ACID STATE OF CHARGE

Battery Condition	State of Charge	12 Volt battery	Volts per Cell
Good	100%	12.7	2.12
	90%	12.5	2.08
	80%	12.42	2.07
	70%	12.32	2.05
	60%	12.2	2.03
OK	50%	12.06	2.01
	40%	11.9	1.98
Unsafe	30%	11.75	1.96
	20%	11.58	1.93
Harmful	10%	11.31	1.89
	0%	10.5	1.75

* The above table depends on the manufacturer and battery type, but most lead-acid batteries will have similar characteristics.

VRLA Batteries require similar charging patterns as flooded lead-acid batteries, but the SOC differs from the voltage in the above table. Lithium-ion batteries also have a distinct voltage pattern for SOC; these are less susceptible to damage from irregular SOC and can be between 20-100% without significantly harming the battery. This means you don't have to recharge the battery to 100% every day or even every week (unlike lead-acid batteries, which need to be recharged to 100% almost every day).

Battery Size Codes

The Battery Council International (BCI) represents the manufacturers of lead-acid batteries. BCI has designated a battery size code in order to group similar batteries together. The code or group ID is based on the physical size and location of the terminals and does not measure the capacity of the batteries. Some batteries have BCI codes and most cases show a list of compatible codes, so you can match the case to the battery.

Off grid solar systems range in size so I can't recommend a specific battery type, but here are some common battery size codes ranging from smaller to larger: U1, 24, 27, 31, T-105, 4-D, 6-D, 8-D. There are some codes that are outdated, such as for floor sweepers "FS" and for golf carts "GC".

Photovoltaic Module Selection

After you've selected your battery system, you should consider which type of Photovoltaic (PV) modules is suitable for your off grid energy system. The batteries determine how long you can provide power when there is no sunshine available, but the PV modules define how much energy you can harvest in your particular location.

PV cells provide instantaneous power and cannot store energy on their own. That is why batteries are frequently used with solar panels in off grid energy systems, so the energy can be utilized when the user needs it.

PV Fundamentals

The power output of a solar module is measured in watts and is equal to the operating voltage multiplied by the operating current. Solar panels produce current over a wide range of voltages. (This is in contrast to batteries, which produce current in a narrow voltage range.) Since a solar panel's voltage can fluctuate significantly, a charge controller can be used to manage the operating voltage and operating current in order to maximize power output. When used with charge controllers, the solar panel's voltage and current are inversely related, so a voltage increase results in a current decrease and vice versa.

Cells, Modules, Panels, and Arrays

The definition of a cell, a module, a panel, and an array is a common area of confusion. They are listed here from smallest to largest.

- **Photovoltaic (PV) cells**: The blue or black 125-150 mm square-shaped silicon wafers that are electrically connected inside of a solar module. There are series and parallel circuits of PV cells inside of the module, which increase the voltage, current and power.
- **PV module**: A collection of PV cells encapsulated in glass and usually housed in an aluminum frame.
- **PV panel**: One or more PV modules preassembled for ease of installation. For example, two modules mounted on a rail with their wires in clips, would be a PV panel.
- **PV array**: The complete power generating system, consisting of any number of PV modules or panels.

Technology Types

There are two main categories of photovoltaic solar modules: crystalline silicon (c-Si) and thin film. Most c-Si PV modules are similar in function and only differ in their efficiency which ranges between 10-22%. On the other hand, thin film PV modules differences are more significant since it is a newer technology.

Mono-Si and Poly-Si

The two types of crystalline silicon PV cells; Monocrystalline (mono-Si) and Polycrystalline (p-Si) are very similar and differ only in the way they are manufactured. Mono-Si PV cells are made from cylinder-shaped ingot crystals sliced into very thin wafers. You can recognize a mono-Si PV module because there are rounded edges near the corner of the cell. Because mono-Si uses purer silicon, it usually has a higher efficiency compared to p-Si.

P-Si crystals are manufactured in a different way, but the end result is still a thin silicon wafer. Raw silicon is heated up until it liquefies, after which it is poured into square molds. The color and texture of the PV cell usually looks purple and iridescent. P-Si is slightly less efficient and slightly less expensive than mono-Si. P-Si modules have slightly less power for the same size module. There are differences in efficiency, price, and power output, but in reality these differences are small.

Thin film

Thin film modules drastically differ from crystalline silicon modules not only in module shape, but also in voltage output, power output, temperature sensitivity, and expected life. Like crystalline silicon modules, there are also many varying types of thin film modules with significantly different manufacturing methods. Mass production of thin film modules started in the early 2000s after a spike in silicon prices drove innovation in lowering quantities of silicon per PV cell.

I would not recommend using thin film for your off grid energy system unless you are very familiar with the product, or are willing to experiment with the advantages and disadvantages of the technology.

Price per Watt

Most PV installers concern themselves more with the price per watt ($/watt) of PV modules than their efficiency. There are many manufacturers of high-quality crystalline Silicon PV modules, and they are all competing to reduce the cost and increase their efficiencies. As long as a company offers a warranty of 25 years and is qualified as a Tier 1 module, you could buy almost any module available in your market with a reasonable expectation of quality and at the lowest available price per watt.

What is Tier 1?

Tier 1 is a ranking scale applied by the Bloomberg New Energy Finance Corporation, which qualifies PV manufacturers based on financial stability and bank-ability. Tier 1 is a process rather than a product standard, confirming the business stability of a module manufacturer rather than the quality of the modules themselves.

Choosing the Right Module Size

PV modules range in size from that of a book to a tabletop. They usually have a higher nominal voltage as the physical size increases. If you are building a small, inexpensive system, you should consider the output voltage of the module to ensure an appropriate match with the rest of the system components. Some PV modules are designed for off grid systems because they have a nominal voltage of 12 V and fluctuate between 0-18 V. 12 V modules are beneficial if you wish to use a less expensive PWM charge controller; larger-format PV modules with 60 or 72 cells will typically have a nominal voltage between 28-36 V and will require MPPT charge controllers (for more, see the *Charge Controller* chapter).

For off grid systems over 3 kW, I recommend using larger PV modules, as they are less expensive per watt. Paired with the more expensive MPPT charge controller, the system can harvest the higher voltage, resulting in a lower overall cost for energy. Also, using larger modules can help you save costs on the racking system and the balance of system components. All of these cost factors should be taken into account when you are collecting your system requirements.

Solar Module Specifications

All solar module manufacturers include a specification sheet or data sheet showing specific details about each module. The next few categories will help you understand what those details mean and how they relate to your system design.

I-V Curve

The power output of a solar panel can be visualized in a performance curve graph otherwise known as an I-V curve (current-voltage). It's shown as a graph with voltage on the horizontal axis and current on the vertical axis (see image on the next page). When a solar module is in the sunlight, it is always functioning on a point on the curve. This curve location will change depending on many conditions, such as the solar irradiance and the ambient temperature. The specification sheet will show an I-V Curve in Standard Test Conditions (STC) — this is not so useful for real world application, but it does give an apples-to-apples comparison between all types of solar modules.

I-V CURVE OVERLAYED WITH P-V CURVE

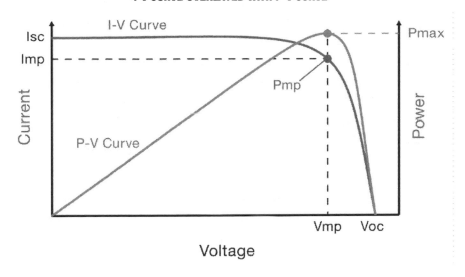

The **Maximum Power Point (Pmp or P$_{max}$)** is equal to Vmp times Imp and is located on the "knee" of the I-V Curve. Maximum Power Point Tracking (MPPT) Charge Controllers can alter the input voltage of a module to harvest the most power from it.

The **Maximum Power Voltage (Vmp)** of a solar panel is typically 70-80% of the maximum open circuit voltage (Voc).

The **Maximum Power Current (Imp)** of a solar panel is typically 90% of the Short Circuit Current (Isc).

The **Open Circuit Voltage (Voc)** is the maximum potential voltage of a module and is on the far right side of an I-V Curve. At Voc there is no power and no current flowing because it represents an "open circuit," meaning the module leads are disconnected. This is like saying the point of the maximum "pressure". The listed Voc on a module's back sheet is based on Standard Test Conditions (STC) and it could potentially be higher under different circumstances, like at lower ambient temperatures.

The **Short Circuit Current (Isc)** is the maximum current if there is no resistance in the circuit. It is located on the far left side of an I-V Curve. A "short circuit" usually means the electrical pathway changed to a shorter path bypassing other components in the circuit resulting in very low resistance and significant current flow. The listed Isc on a module's back sheet is based on STC and represents the maximum potential current flow in the module.

Standard Test Conditions (STC)

Standard Test Conditions (STC) represents the solar industry standard for measuring the performance of a solar module. It provides a fair comparison between different solar module manufacturers. The variables affecting the performance of a solar module are the temperature of the cells, the solar irradiance, and the mass of the air. STC is when the cell temperature is 25° C with a solar irradiance of 1000 Watts per square meter and 1.5 mass of air. The 1.5 mass of air is a coefficient representing a diagonal path through the atmosphere compared to a directly vertical one. These conditions were designed to represent a clear sunny day for most places on earth.

The Effects of Module Shading

Most people do not realize that a small amount of shading on the modules can dramatically reduce the production of a solar array. For example, shading 10% of the array area could reduce the production of the whole system by 50%. Moreover, if a module does not have **Bypass Diodes**, then shading one PV cell could result in power loss of up to 75%! There should ideally be no shading for six hours during the sunniest part of the day over the entire year. However, this is not always possible, so reducing shade during the middle part of the day remains paramount.

Some solar modules have bypass diodes that help redirect the flow of electricity when a portion of the PV cells are in the shade. Generally, solar module's cells are connected in series, so all the electricity produced in one cell needs to travel through all the other cells before exiting the solar panel. If a cell downstream is shaded, the voltage drops due to increased resistance, and all of the cells in the rest of the series have diminished power.

Bypass diodes can be found inside the junction box of most solar modules. They work along with the modules' PV cells to effectively redirect the current inside the module, providing it with another path to travel should shading occur. Most large solar modules have replaceable bypass diodes inside the junction box on the back. Since opening the junction box can void the module warranty, check with your owner's manual before doing so.

Below is a diagram that shows how the electricity will flow when there is partial shading on the solar panel. With a PV module that has three bypass diodes, partial shading of just one cell can drop the module output by one third. This diagram is a birds-eye-view showing an object, like a roof vent, that casts a shadow on the solar panel at different times of the day.

EXAMPLE OF THE EFFECTS OF SHADE

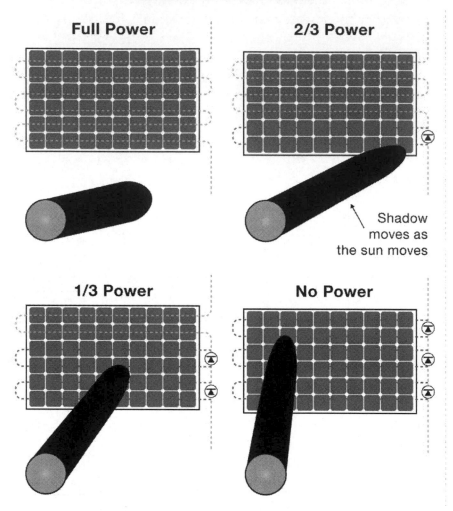

If you place multiple rows of tilted solar modules on the ground or on a flat roof, be sure to include enough space between modules to account for exposure during the six peak sun hours of the day. Consider the sun angle during the peak sun hours in the winter and ensure that production is sufficient for your system.

Generally, Inter-Row Spacing should be approximately 1.5–2 times the Array Height, but this changes depending on your site conditions. Below is an image showing how a smaller Sun Angle means it is more necessary to have a longer Inter-Row Spacing.

INTER-ROW SPACING DIAGRAM

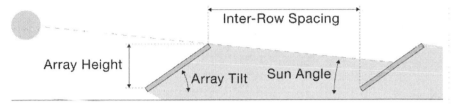

Strings of Modules

In the *Battery* chapter, I explained how to connect batteries in series by plugging a positive lead of one battery to a negative lead of another; the same thing goes for solar modules. By connecting modules in series, you are adding to the voltage while maintaining the same current. Connecting modules in series like this creates a string. Use the same type of modules in a string whenever possible in order to maintain high efficiencies. You should not typically connect different solar panels in the same string, but it is acceptable so long as they have similar current ratings. If you connect dissimilar modules together in series, the string will be reduced to the module with the lowest amperage; in other words, the amperage will only be as strong as the weakest link in the string.

On the next page is an image showing how two modules connected together will have matching power output, but with different voltage or current depending on which type of connection is in place. It's worth reiterating here that in a series connection, you have double the voltage, but the current remains the same. In a parallel connection, you have double the current, but the voltage remains the same.

SERIES VS. PARALLEL CONNECTION METHOD

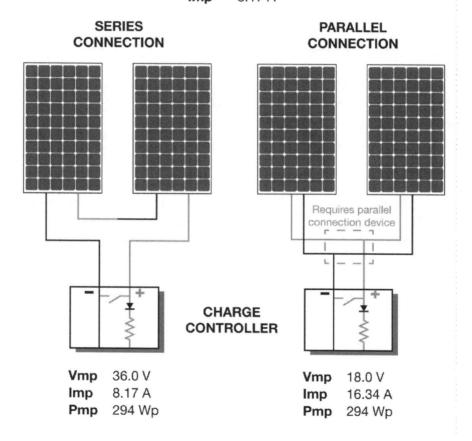

PV MODULE SPEC SHEET

Pmax	145 Wp
Voc	22.2 V
Vmp	18.0 V
Isc	8.69 A
Imp	8.17 A

SERIES CONNECTION

PARALLEL CONNECTION

Requires parallel connection device

CHARGE CONTROLLER

Vmp	36.0 V
Imp	8.17 A
Pmp	294 Wp

Vmp	18.0 V
Imp	16.34 A
Pmp	294 Wp

Strings can range from two up to 20 or more modules depending on how the DC electronics are designed. Typically you will string together as many modules as possible into a series connection until the desired voltage is reached. At that point, if more modules are desired, you can add more strings with the same number of modules in parallel to the other strings until reaching the current you want.

Remember that parallel connections of PV modules require a parallel connection device such as an outdoor combiner box or outdoor rated Y-combiner. A combiner box with DIN rail terminals or Polaris boxes would be sufficient to terminate the conductors. Series connections are usually male-to-female, and they do not need any connection terminal.

It is very important that the open circuit voltage (Voc) of your string of modules does not exceed the input voltage of the charge controller or other DC electronics. Add up the Voc of all your modules in series and compare that to the input voltage of your equipment while keeping in mind that the extreme temperatures in your site location can alter the Voc.

The Effects of Temperature

When a solar module's cell temperature exceeds 25 °C, the power output will drop below its nameplate performance. Solar cells function less efficiently under higher temperatures because the heat adds resistance to the flow of electrons. For every degree above 25 °C, the module's performance will drop by approximately 0.5%. In very cold climates, the opposite is true: it's even possible to outperform the STC power output on very bright winter days due to the reduced internal resistance.

PV Array Maximum Voltage for Cold Climates

Outperforming the STC power output presents its own set of concerns. Since the module power can increase on those bright cold days, you must ensure that the string of modules will not exceed the voltage limits of the rest of the system. Exceeding the voltage limits will destroy electronics. Fuses and circuit breakers only protect from high current, not voltage!

Solar panels have a wide voltage range and this can get very high on bright, cold days. Most module manufacturers will list a temperature coefficient for the open circuit voltage (TC_{Voc}) and the short circuit current (TC_{Isc}). It will be listed as volts per °C or percentage per ° C below 25 °C. You should always determine the extreme minimum temperature, not the average.

If, for example, the lowest recorded temperature in your region was -10 °C, then the difference from STC conditions would be 35 °C. If a PV module has a Voc of 37.2V and a TC_{Voc} of -0.34%/°C, then the calculation below shows that the adjusted Voc would be 41.6V for that module.

$$TC_{Voc} \times (25°C - lowest\ recorded\ temp.) = \%\ Adjustment$$

$$-0.34\%/°C \times (25°C - (-10°C)) = -11.9\%$$

$$Voc\ at\ STC \times (1 - (\%\ Adjustment)) = Adjusted\ Voc$$

$$37.2\ V \times (1 - (-11.9\%)) = 41.6\ V$$

Charge Controller Selection

Charge controllers act like energy managers, protecting the battery and optimizing the energy generated by the solar panels. The electronics inside are designed to only let electricity flow under certain circumstances, and to protect the batteries.

Sometimes called DC-DC converters, regulators, or power trackers, charge controllers serve as protection devices connecting the solar panels and the batteries. Charge controllers modify the voltage from the solar panels throughout the charging cycle of the batteries and provide the required charging voltage depending on the charging stage. They also have some protections in place, such as a low-voltage battery disconnect and overcharge protection. Not all charge controllers have the same features or efficiency, so be sure to research your options before choosing.

PWM or MPPT?

All charge controllers have a variety of features that protect the system, but their main purpose is to handle the solar power and transfer it to the batteries in a safe and efficient manner. Charge controllers fall into two major categories: **Pulse Width Modulation** (PWM) and **Maximum Power Point Tracking** (MPPT). Deciding between the two types depends greatly on the size of the system, the Voc of your solar panel(s), and your local climate.

MPPT charge controllers are more complex and more efficient, but also more expensive than PWM controllers. Their electronics allow them to operate at the Maximum Power Voltage (Vmp) of the solar modules, allowing for 5-25% more efficiency (especially when PV voltage is over 150 V). Also, larger solar modules with 60 or 72 cells typically have a higher operating voltage than the battery voltage. In this case, an MPPT charge controller becomes more cost effective because the electronics harvest more solar energy by converting all of that extra voltage into current.

PWM charge controllers never operate at Vmp and they "pull down" the voltage to what the battery requires by clipping all the excess voltage. The PWM charge controller's simple electronics do not convert that larger voltage potential into current. The PV modules designed for off grid applications that typically have 36 cells are compatible with PWM and MPPT controllers, but the larger modules might not match the voltage with the PWM controller.

PWM VS. MPPT ON I-V CURVE

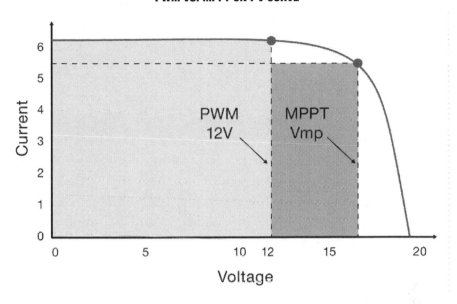

The graph above shows how the MPPT harvests the most power available by tracking the voltage and current to the Vmp point on the "knee" of the IV curve. Notice how the PWM doesn't track the voltage or current, but instead pushes the voltage back to 12 V?

Considerations with PWM

A PWM charge controller might be the best option if:
1. The solar array is small with only a few modules;
2. The module nominal voltage is slightly above but close to the battery voltage;
3. You are in a warm climate.

For example, if you are using a 12 V nominal (0-18 V) solar panel with a 12 V nominal (12-14 V) battery system, then the solar panel will usually provide just the right voltage needed to charge the batteries without sacrificing very much efficiency. This is because in warmer climates, a 12 V nominal

(0-18 V) module will have voltage drop due to internal resistance. As a result, it will typically have a voltage in the range of what the battery needs (12-14V). This system would not gain from the advantages provided by the more complex MPPT charge controller.

On the other hand, the same system in colder climates might have a voltage closer to 18 V during cold and sunny days. The PWM controller would "push" that voltage down to 12 V, meaning the current would stay the same and the power would be relatively low. Alternatively, with an MPPT controller that extra voltage above 12 V would convert to current and the system would be functioning at Pmp. Because of this, the increased power during those cold sunny days might justify the cost for a MPPT charge controller.

If you plan on running long wires or using thin wires from the solar to the charge controller or batteries, the voltage will drop from the increased resistance. This could drop the voltage below the charging voltage of the batteries. A PWM controller is unable to push up the voltage to what the battery requires; however, an MPPT controller could handle the voltage drop.

Considerations with MPPT

Not all MPPT charge controllers the same; look for trusted brands with useful warranties and a strong reputation. The effectiveness of the MPPT electronics can vary significantly. MPPT electronics sweep through the I-V curve searching for the highest power output and lock into the Maximum Power Point for peak efficiency. The speed of the sweep and the number of times the sweep is initiated is completely up to the designers of the MPPT controller. Some low-quality controllers might take a full minute to complete a sweep of the I-V curve and might only initiate it a few times a day. The better brands can sweep in as fast as 0.25 seconds and will initiate the sweep much more often.

All of these examples show that the complexities of MPPT help increase solar energy harvesting, but with an added cost as well. You will need to make the final decision as to whether or not the benefits outweigh the costs for your project.

Matching to Battery Type

Most Charge Controllers offer an option for charging sealed or flooded lead-acid batteries, and it is important to configure them to match your battery type. Few of them have predetermined settings for lithium batteries and require custom configuration to work properly. Properly configuring a charge controller will keep the battery maximum and minimum voltage set points and the rate for charging/discharging properly synced, helping to extend battery life, and keeping the system safe.

Lithium-ion batteries are relatively new for off grid solar, which means only a few charge controllers are designed for them. Also, some lithium-ion Battery Management Systems might need to communicate with the charge controller or inverter in order to avoid unexpected disconnections. Ensure that the communication line can trigger the BMS to reconnect with the battery after a disconnection. For example, if the SOC drops below a certain threshold, the BMS will disconnect from the load to protect the battery, which could result in the battery not being charged.

Visit my website for more details on charge controllers that are compatible with lithium-ion batteries.

www.OffGridSolarBook.com/Store

System Protection

In order to protect all of the equipment in the circuit, charge controllers have electronics that set the protocol to open or close pathways depending on voltages and direction of flow.

Disconnects

Since batteries can be severely damaged if the voltage drops below 20% state of charge, a Low Voltage Disconnect (LVD) can disconnect the battery from the load to avoid permanent damage. Batteries can also be damaged if they are overcharged, so charge controllers usually also have an Overcharge Protection that cuts the PV supply to the batteries when they reach maximum charge.

Since electricity flows via the path of least resistance, it is possible for the battery to push current back into the solar array. PV modules are not designed to have electricity flow back into them, so a reversal of current could prove disastrous. Charge Controllers will typically have a Reverse Current Protection to protect the PV array.

In spite of these protections built into the charge controller, it is not safe to just hook up any assortment of PV modules, batteries and loads. For example, most charge controllers do not have any protection from a high voltage input from the solar array, so the system designer should plan the system based on the worst-case Voc of the PV array.

Check the specification sheet of the charge controller for which protection features are present as well as their parameters, which may be adjusted to suit your system requirements.

Temperature Compensation

Some charge controllers will alter their charge characteristics depending on the ambient temperature of the batteries. This is particularly important for sealed batteries due to their greater sensitivity to overcharging. Temperature Compensation is most effective when the temperature swings more than 10 °C in the course of a year. This will ensure full charge in the winter months and prevent overcharging in the summer months.

Equalization Charging

With flooded batteries, the different cells will periodically have unbalanced charges, and an equalization charge is needed to restore equal charges among cells. This will also reduce sulfation and stratification. Some charge controllers have automatic or manual equalization charging. Flooded lead-acid batteries should be equalized once or twice every month to maintain their life. When using lithium batteries, always turn off the equalizing option.

CHARGE CONTROLLER DAILY CHARGE PROFILE FOR

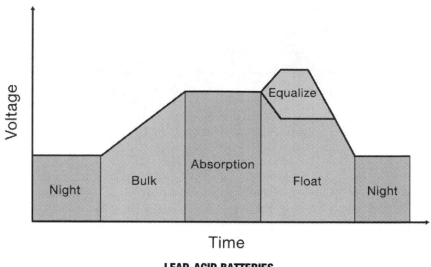

LEAD-ACID BATTERIES

Note that the equalize stage will not happen every day.

Inverter Selection

For off grid solar systems, inverters are needed to change the DC power coming from the batteries and the solar panels into AC power for final use. The only systems that need an inverter are those in which some of the equipment runs on AC.

For smaller systems the solar charge controller tends to be the brains of the system, but for larger systems the inverter does all the sensing and communicating between components. Some manufacturers even combine the charge controller and the inverter into one unit for simplicity in the installation process.

Inverter Fundamentals

Electricity, or current, can flow in two ways: alternating current (AC) or direct current (DC). The difference between AC and DC is the direction of flow; DC always flows in one direction while AC flows rapidly back and forth at a specific frequency measured in Hertz (Hz). AC is best for transmission over long distances and is the standard for grid electricity. Direct current is typically used for short distances, and, since it doesn't alternate, has no frequency in Hertz. Batteries and solar panels naturally flow in DC. Most electronics such as cell phones, computers, LED lights, and televisions function in DC, so they require an AC to DC converter with AC grids.

So, why bother with AC if everything runs off of DC? You could build your solar energy system and power your home all in DC without the need of an inverter, but you would need to use appliances that are designed for DC input. A greater challenge, though, is that you will also still need to match your system voltage to your electronic devices. For transmitting energy over long distances, it's advantageous to use a high voltage system to reduce losses from resistance; otherwise, you will need thick (expensive) wiring. High voltage reduces the resistance and allows you to use smaller, less expensive wire. Currently, no common standard has been set for DC voltages in a home, so getting the right transformer to step down the voltage to the level needed for your electrical devices is not easy or always possible. Because of this, most off grid systems will decide on a DC to AC inverter for transmission to the home and then use AC to DC converters for each electronic device.

Match to the Utility in Your Country

Even if you are building an off grid system, it is wise to match your inverter to your country's plug type, voltage, and frequency, as designated by the utility grids of your locale. There are 15 types of electrical outlet plugs used around the world today, but universal plug adapters can only be matched to your receptacle outlets. The important thing is to select appliances that are compatible with the voltage and the frequency; the plug shape does not really matter. In most parts of the world a standard plug outlet is between 220-240 V and 50 Hz, but the Americas and parts of Asia are 100-127 V and 60 Hz. Mismatched electrical equipment may not function properly, and it could prove unsafe to use the wrong voltage and frequency. Check with the manufacturer, because some products are designed to work with both types of power even though the outlet plugs do not match.

Power: Continuous vs. Surge

Inverters have a designated power rating for continuous use and a larger power rating for a short surge. The surge is typically no more than double the continuous load and rated for a limited amount of time, but each manufacturer has different specifications. For example, a 300-watt inverter might have a 600-watt surge at 5 seconds. The surge power matters quite a lot if you are using motors, transformers, or capacitors on the load side of your system. (This includes refrigerators, vacuums, power tools, pumps, and camera flashes.) The surge or inrush current on motors is generally more than double their continuous load, so don't assume a motor will work with your inverter just because the continuous power matches.

Surge Power cannot be measured with a regular multimeter or Kill A Watt meter, so if you need to determine the surge of a motor, you will need an oscilloscope or at least a clamp meter with an inrush current setting.

System Protection

Like charge controllers, inverters also house electronics meant to protect the equipment in a circuit by a set of protocols that open or close pathways depending on voltage and direction of flow. Some inverters have features that protect the equipment in the circuit from over current and high temperatures.

Dealing with Power Factor

In AC circuits, the Power Factor (PF) can affect the quality of the power provided. PF is the ratio of the real power that is used to do work and the apparent power that is supplied to the circuit. PF thus represents the quality of the power provided and ranges from 0 (bad) to 1 (good).

When the PF is low and approaching zero, there is significant inductive load (otherwise known as reactive power). Appliances that use magnetic energy to work cause inductive loads, such as motors and transformers. You can spot these appliances without much trouble since the large coils of wire needed to use magnetic energy make them quite heavy.

When the PF is high and close to 1, all the power is real with little reactive power. This occurs with resistive load. Resistive loads typically are used to convert electricity into heat, such as in electric heaters and incandescent bulbs.

If you have a lot of motors in your system, the power factor could drop too low, causing the system to function improperly and overheat. You can test a circuit's power factor with a Kill A Watt meter. Consider enlarging your inverter or getting rid of the appliance in question if you test your circuit and the PF is below 0.9. I would not recommend using Power Factor correction devices since I have never heard of one functioning properly.

Pure Sine Wave vs. Modified Wave

As with charge controllers, there are two distinct types of inverters: the Pure Sine Wave and the Modified Wave. The image below shows how the two differ in alternating the current in an AC circuit.

Because the modified sine wave abruptly shifts the direction of the current, it can harm some equipment it powers. Almost all electronic devices, like computers, TVs, battery chargers, LED or fluorescent lights, digital clocks, digital radios, etc., are negatively affected by modified sine wave inverters. These products will either not work, overheat, malfunction during use, or have their usable lives shortened. Devices like resistant heaters and motors with brushes would work fine with a modified sine wave inverter.

For almost all cases, a pure sine wave inverter is the best option. It is very hard to predict how the products on the load side will react to the modified sine wave inverter.

COMPARING SINE TO MODIFIED WAVE

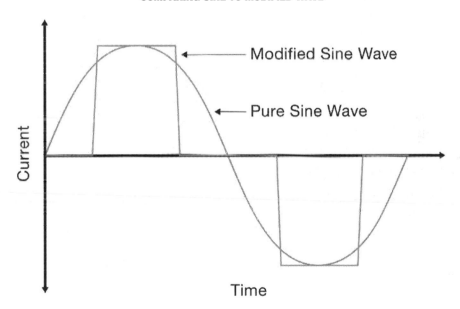

Single Phase, Split Phase and Three-Phase

If you are building a system under 5 kilowatts, you will most likely want a Single Phase inverter. Split Phase and Three-Phase inverters have additional circuits that share a neutral path for additional power, resulting in fewer redundant conductors. Split Phase is common for homes in North America and Three-Phase is common for larger commercial systems.

If your system is smaller than 5 kilowatts of peak power, you should plan to use a single phase inverter since these other types are typically only used for on-grid applications or larger systems. If your project is significantly large (above 5 kilowatts) you might consider a split phase inverter if you are in North America, but this depends on how you will manage your loads panel.

If you are building a microgrid and you have long wire runs, using a Three-Phase inverter would be advantageous. Because with three-phase systems you have three wires that share a common neutral wire, so you can have three circuits with four wires which saves on wire costs.

Bi-Directional Inverters

As discussed, inverters convert direct current (DC) to alternating current (AC), to render solar or battery power into energy usable for your home. But in some circumstances, it is useful, also, to be able to convert AC to DC as well (for example, to use a generator to charge batteries on cloudy winter days). AC to DC conversion is called rectifying; a rectifier changes AC to DC.

A **Bi-Directional Inverter**, also called a Hybrid or Battery Inverter, converts both directions between DC and AC. It can rectify (convert from AC to DC) and invert the power (convert from DC to AC). All that means is that the inverter also has a battery charger built into it. Some of these solar battery inverters also have the ability to convert high voltage DC from the solar array to a lower voltage for the battery. In this case it is simply an inverter with a battery charger and a charge controller in one box. It could be beneficial to buy all of these components in one box rather than have three separate components.

Also, many of these inverters are designed for lead-acid batteries and need to be custom configured for lithium-ion batteries. Visit my website for more details on selecting a compatible inverter for use with lithium-ion batteries.

www.OffGridSolarBook.com/Store

Inverter Efficiency

Not all inverters have the same efficiency of converting from DC to AC and DC to AC power. Often inverters state their peak efficiency, but it is more important to understand the full efficiency curve. See example below.

EXAMPLE INVERTER EFFICIENCY CURVE

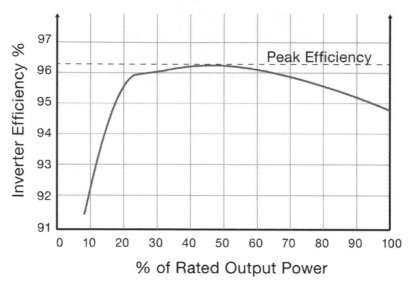

For most inverters the efficiency is very low when inverting lower power. For off grid systems it is really important to understand the efficiency at low power, because it can drain the batteries faster than you might have estimated. For example, if you are powering a 100-watt LED light with an inverter that has a maximum power of 5,000 watts, then you are only using small portion of the inverter's capacity. The inverter efficiency might be 65% at that low power even though its peak efficiency is around 96%. That means the inverter needs to invert 154 watts of DC power to provide 100 watts of AC power for that LED light. If you expect to frequently use your inverter at or below 20% of its rated power, then you should review inverter operation manuals to identify one with the highest efficiency at low power, taking into account that low power used for many hours will add up quickly.

Because of the efficiency differences between inverters, it would be more realistic to compare them with a weighted efficiency. To do this you would need to consider both the typical solar production power ranges to estimate the charging range, and the typical load power ranges to estimate the inverter range. This is specific to your solar configuration and your system load profile – or in other words, specific to how often you are using power at each efficiency range.

Standby or Idle Power

Beyond energy wasted due to poor efficiency while converting low power, the inverter also uses a measurable amount of standby power when not in active use. Consider this the energy needed for the inverter to be on, warmed up, and ready to work. Some inverters may use up to 30 watts as a baseline, even though they are not inverting or charging. This standby power, also called idle, tare, or no-load power, can be a big drain on your battery system, since it may be on 24 hours a day. It would be wise to factor it into one of the loads on your load calculation table discussed in the *Site Design* chapter.

Power Save Mode

Many inverters have a "power save" mode where the inverter turns off or hibernates, reducing the standby power while waiting for a trigger to reactivate. This mode might also be called silent or search mode. There are many ways the inverter can reduce its power consumption, but some inverters turn off in multiple stages, leaving one stage active; while others reduce the available voltage down to the minimum until a power threshold is reached (for example 100 watts). Many times this power save mode is disabled by default, so be sure to turn it on, if relevant.

If the minimum threshold is set too high, then some loads may not work when the inverter is triggered into power save mode. So if you plan to have some low power systems operating such as security systems or clocks, the inverter may never drop below the threshold and never enter into power save mode. For those small loads, it might be better to use small rechargeable batteries inside the device or even another smaller always-on inverter that is dedicated to them.

Passively-Cooled Versus Fan-Cooled

All of the electronics in an off grid solar system get hot when they are used, and solar equipment tends to be sited in sunny locations, so extreme heat can cause real problems. Some inverter and charge controller manufacturers allow you to place their equipment in direct sunlight, but it doesn't mean you should. Cooler inside temperatures, as long as they are above freezing, will generally help the electronics run more efficiently and contribute to a longer lifespan. Check the instruction manual to see the appropriate operating temperatures.

Inverters and charge controllers need to remove the heat from their components to maintain efficiencies and avoid damage. This is most often done with fans that pull outside air into the equipment. If your equipment will be set up in a particularly dusty or corrosive environment, such as near the ocean, be very careful if using fans as cooling systems. It might be better to purchase a passively-cooled system with a heat sink for both the inverter and charge controller. Large metal fins inside a passively-cooled system radiate the heat off of the electronics and into the surrounding air. Passively-cooled electronics require no electricity to move air around and instead use heat convection. Because of this, passively-cooled equipment can be fully sealed to protect from dust or corrosive air.

Balance of System Selection

Balance of System (BOS) commonly refers to all mechanical and electrical equipment and hardware other than the major components, which are needed to finish the installation. These include conductors (wiring), wire management devices (like raceways and conduits), junction and combiner boxes, disconnect switches, fuses and circuit breakers, terminals and connectors, grounding, and mounting hardware. Even minor components play essential roles in the efficient, lasting operation of your off grid system, so understanding how they work and how to choose the proper kinds for your specific needs is imperative.

Wire Selection

A wire used for electrical systems is usually made of a copper or aluminum conductor with or without a protective sleeve. In everyday speech, the terms "wire" and "cable" are often used interchangeably. They have a distinct difference: a wire has one conductor and a cable bundles together two or more wires inside a single sleeve.

The conductor inside of a single wire can be solid metal or it can consist of multiple stranded wires braided together with insulation around them making a single conductor. Braided wires are more flexible, making them easier to work with compared to the solid metal type of wires.

The protective sleeve (a.k.a. sheathing) on a cable or a wire is there to insulate it from other conductors and to protect it from the elements. Some sleeves protect from water, ultraviolet light, high heat or fire, and/or corrosive environments. Not all sleeves are the same, so be sure to check which environments the sleeve is designed for.

Selection of the correct conductors for the job is too often left as an afterthought. Proper wire gauge is critical for an efficient and safe energy system.

Copper is commonly used as the conductor but occasionally aluminum is used to save on material cost. For the same gauge of wire, the diameter cross section of copper will be smaller than aluminum, because it inherently has less resistance as a material property.

As wire standards can differ by region, you should get familiar with local codes. In North America, the American Wire Gauge (AWG) is predominantly used. If you do not have a prevailing local code, then your best choice will be IEC 60228, the international standard on conductors of insulated cables created by the International Electrotechnical Commission (IEC). It defines standard wire cross-section areas in mm^2. For a quick reference, let's go through a few of the most widely used types of wire.

Common Wire Types

Based on American Wire Gauge (AWG) and Underwriters Laboratories (UL):

- **PV:** Designed to be used to connect photovoltaic modules together into strings. Its sheathing is resistant to UV exposure and can be buried.
- **THHN/THWN:** Primarily used inside of conduit and cable trays, thermoplastic insulation with nylon sleeve. Not UV resistant.
- **USE/UF:** Designed for underground use and should be buried 300-600 mm deep. The PVC sleeve of USE/UF wiring is fungus resistant and can be exposed to water.
- **RHH/RHW:** Rubber insulated wire used for connecting batteries.
- **NM (aka Romex®):** Usually a two or three conductor cable with a PVC sleeve. Used for AC wire in the interior of a house.

Electrical Resistance

Selecting the correct conductor (wire) for the job depends on a variety of conditions, but the most important thing to remember is that while all wires have some amount of resistance, this should be kept to a minimum. The wire gauge is proportional to the maximum current acceptable. High resistance equals loss of power and increased heat. The wire gauge should be predetermined by the maximum current a wire will carry with an acceptable amount of line resistance.

Wiring is not an area in which you should cut corners. Trying to save money by using thinner wire than required will result in loss of power and could actually cost you more money in the long run. Also, a wire that's too thin won't be able to properly conduct the high current traveling through its small diameter, creating enough added heat that the insulation could melt and even cause a fire. This could be a dangerous mistake, so make sure you are following the requirements of your local code.

Conductor Sizing Calculations

Since the goal is to minimize resistance in the wires, set a few guidelines to avoid an excessive drop in voltage. Depending on where the conductor is in the circuit, the voltage drop due to conductor resistance should be calculated and appropriate for each circuit.

Voltage Drop $= I \times \Omega$

When choosing the correct conductor, you must determine the maximum current in the circuit, the size of the fuses or breakers, the ambient temperature, and the material type of the conductor and insulation. With this information, you can make a calculated decision concerning the proper gauge and type of wire. Keep in mind that if you plan on grouping many conductors inside of conduit or in an enclosed wire tray, this will change the ambient temperature. It is also important to make sure that the terminal connections and end connectors are not the highest points of resistance. Some equipment might have a required torque value on the fasteners in order to minimize unintended resistance.

To calculate the voltage drop based on your project parameters, use the voltage drop calculator on my website.

www.OffGridSolarBook.com/Resources

Distinct Circuits in an Off Grid PV System

Unfortunately, you can't use the same wire for the entire job. There are many circuits within an off grid solar system and it's helpful to map out the entire system into subcircuits. Some of those circuits are DC while others might be AC. There are circuits with different voltage and current requirements, and with varying length and weather exposure. The entire system should be viewed in each circuit scenario.

The diagram below shows a basic example of the subcircuits in a complete off grid PV system:

- **PV Source**: PV modules to combiner box
  - Common wire type: PV wire
- **PV Output**: PV combiner box to charge controller
  - Common wire type: PV wire, THHN/THWN within EMT conduit, or USE/UF for underground
- **Battery Input**: Charge controller to batteries
  - Common wire type: RHH/RHW wire
- **Inverter Output**: Inverter to AC loads
  - Common wire type: NM or Romex wire

BASIC SUBCIRCUITS OF AN OFF GRID PV SYSTEM

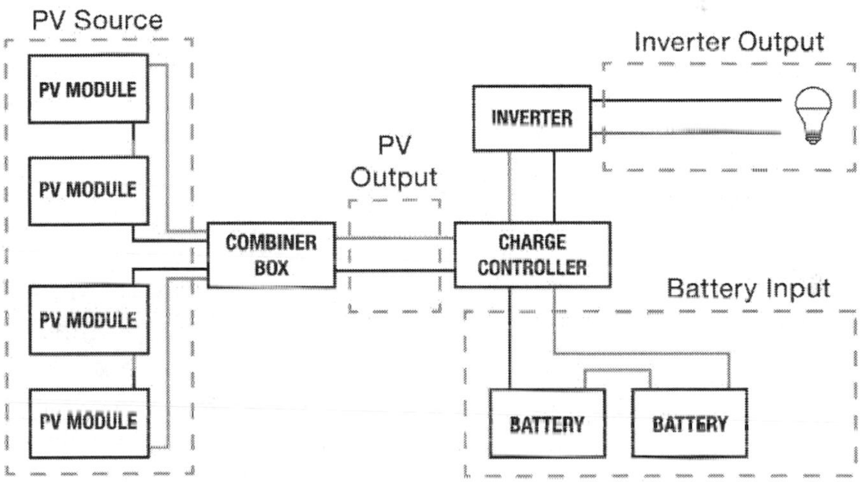

PV Source Circuit

This circuit connects the modules together into strings and terminates at a combiner box or the charge controller. When in doubt, select the same wire size and connectors as the system modules. PV wire works well in outdoor environments and for some sun exposure.

The wire requirements for the PV source are dependent on the module's listed short-circuit current (Isc). To calculate this, find the module's rated short-circuit current and multiply it by 1.25. This will give you the maximum current for that circuit. The maximum current in the system is determined by 125% because it is possible for the modules to outperform their STC short-circuit rating. If you have one string going to the inverter and the modules have a rated Isc of 8.41 A, then the PV source maximum current is:

$$Imax = 8.41\,A \times 1.25 = 10.5\,A$$

PV Output Circuit

If you plan on combining strings of modules **in parallel** to a combiner box, then you might need to step up the wire gauge, change to underground cable, or change wire type for conduit. Whenever modules are connected in parallel the current is added up, which typically requires the wire size to increase.

If you plan to have more than one string of modules, combine them in parallel inside of a combiner box near the modules. The PV Output maximum current establishes what the conductor size should be from the combiner box to the charge controller. Find the sum of the total short-circuit current for each of the strings and multiply them by 1.25. For example, if you have two strings going to the combiner box and the modules have a rated Isc of 8.41 A, then the PV source maximum current is (8.41 A + 8.41 A) * 1.25 = 21.0 A.

The PV circuit should have Overcurrent Protection Devices (OCPDs) such as fuses or breakers, which will protect the components in their circuit. It will typically need to be 125% higher than the Imax of all the PV modules.

$$OCPD = Imax \times 1.25 = 21.0\,A \times 1.25 = 26.3\,A$$

Battery Input Circuit

The wire used between the batteries is usually the largest wire in your system, because batteries move a large amount of current at a low voltage. Additionally, they can be exposed to high temperatures, sulfuric acid, and hydrogen gas, so they need a sufficient gauge conductor as well as a suitable insulation for the environment. For a 12-48 V battery array with over 100 Ah of capacity, for example, the wire gauge might be 2/0 to 4/0 AWG, which is equivalent to 70 to 120 cross section mm². Assuming the distance is fewer than 3 meters (10 feet), a maximum current of 175 A is suitable for 2/0 AWG conductors and a maximum current of 250 A is suitable for 4/0 AWG conductors. Automotive or welding cables are obviously designed for a different purpose, but they might be sufficient for your system in this case. Also, welding cables are easy to work with because they are made of finely braided thin wires, which makes them very flexible.

It is important to use appropriate ring terminal connectors and to crimp them properly. Tighten the nut onto the lug terminal according to the battery specifications. The longest-lasting lugs are made from copper. (It's possible to use steel and aluminum lugs, but they will corrode quickly due to the dissimilar metals in contact.) Use closed-ended lugs, as open-ended ones will enable corrosion to enter into the strands of the wire.

CLOSED END LUG

Poorly crimped cables could potentially spark or short circuit.
Combine that with an environment containing hydrogen gas
from flooded lead-acid batteries, and you have an extremely
dangerous situation. Either purchase the battery cables
preassembled with lugs pre-cut to size, or purchase a high-
quality crimper tool designed for that particular connector
and gauge of wire.

EXAMPLE OF A GOOD CRIMP

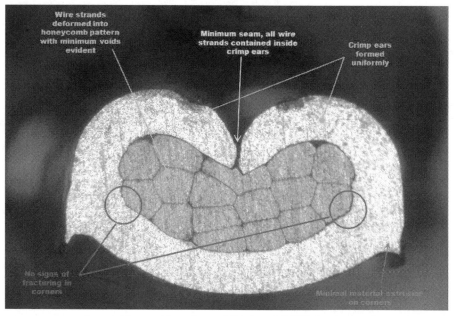

Source: Cross-section of a good F-crimp, ETCO Incorporated

Inverter Output Circuit

The output of the inverter can connect directly to your AC electrical equipment, or it can connect to a load center that distributes the electricity to branch circuits. The inverter output is either 220-240 V or 100-127 V, depending on your system design. With higher voltage on the AC side of the circuit, current is lower for the same amount of power, allowing for smaller wire sizes or longer runs. This makes it easier to distribute and branch off wires and distribute to the end-use loads.

You will most likely need wire gauges between 14 to 10 AWG (2.5 to 6.0 mm^2) for a 120-Vac system. The same calculations which determine the maximum current for the PV circuit and battery circuit apply to the AC side of the system, and remember to keep resistance to a minimum. If you run a thin wire a long distance from your inverter, then the resistance will increase, resulting in a voltage drop. Should the voltage drop too much, the end-use equipment might not work properly. Ideally, you want to ensure that the voltage drop in the inverter output circuit never exceeds 5% for branch circuits and 3% for feeder circuits. Feeder circuits are near the source of energy and carry the full load of the system, while branch circuits are subcircuits of the system providing lower power than the full system.

Overcurrent Protection Devices

An Overcurrent Protection Device (OCPD) protects a circuit experiencing an unusually high surge of current from an overload, short circuit, or a ground fault. It is often forgotten that OCPDs are there to protect the conductors, not the equipment. Typically, equipment has internal fuses to protect from high surge current. OCPDs are the most fundamental requirement in any electrical system and are designed to protect from the following:

- An **overload** is a situation where equipment is used and it exceeds the rated capacity of the circuit.
- A **short circuit** is an unintended electrical connection between any two current-carrying conductors, and is referring to shortening the path in a circuit.
- A **ground fault** is an unintended electrical connection between an ungrounded conductor of a circuit and the grounding conductor or any other metal component like the racking system.

Common OCPDs, like fuses or circuit breakers, disconnect the circuit when currents exceed their rated capacity for a rated duration of time. **Fuses** no longer function after being "blown" by a power surge. You will have to replace them with a new one every time a surge occurs. However, **Circuit Breakers** can be reused and are commonly used as a disconnect device because they can be turned on and off like a switch without the need for replacement.

In order for any OCPD to function properly, it must have a rated capacity equal to or less than the conductor to which it's connected. OCPDs protect conductors; they won't necessarily do anything for other equipment in the system. That said, some equipment does have built-in overcurrent protection to protect its internal components. Despite that protection, any conductors connecting to components in your system will still need an OCPD. When purchasing your OCPD, be sure to match the termination type and the range of wire gauges to your system design.

Combiner Boxes and Disconnects

Whenever you have parallel connections, you will need a way to combine the many wires into fewer wires. For example, if you have 3 strings of PV modules and only one PV input on your charge controller, how will you terminate the wires if there is no room to land them? In this case, you need to reduce 3 positive and 3 negative wires to where there is only one positive and one negative slot. Using terminal connectors with jumpers, bus-bars, or terminal blocks is a way to bond multiple wires together. But you will also need an enclosure to protect the connections from the outdoor environment.

A **Combiner Box** is nothing more than a place to safely combine parallel connections of conductors. It has a hole with watertight cord grips for wires to go inside with some way to combine the conductors, such as DIN rail mounted terminals or bus bars for the positive and negative conductors. Typically there are some OCPDs or a disconnect switch inside the box as well.

A **Disconnect** is a device that opens the circuit to stop the flow of electricity. They allow you to isolate equipment in case of emergency, repair, or maintenance. Sometimes a combiner box can function as a disconnect as well. The PV array and batteries should each have their own disconnect: either a disconnect switch or circuit breakers. Other energy sources such as a generator should also have a disconnect, but sometimes these have a built-in on/off switch.

Grounding

There are many things that can go wrong with an off grid energy system, and equipment grounding is a form of insurance for when something does go wrong. All electrical components need to be electrically connected to earth, i.e., grounded, in case any part of the system's components gets energized. Grounding reduces the chance of electrical shock, allows the OCPD to trip in the event of a short circuit, and can also protect the system from lightning strikes.

A properly grounded PV system electrically connects all the electrically conductive parts, so they have the same potential voltage compared to earth. The module frame, racking, conduit, metal boxes and all other metal equipment should be electrically connected with a bare copper or silver conductor thick enough to handle a surge of the OCPD in line with it.

The equipment you purchase will have instruction manuals with recommendations on how to properly ground your system. Typically, you would connect the grounding wire to the grounding terminal block in the DC circuit breaker box, and then connect a larger wire to a grounding rod or some other ground source, like a ground water pipe. The negative conductor should be connected either to the ground fault protection or to the grounding terminal block between the battery and the charge controller. It's important that the grounding connection to the negative conductor happens in only one place; otherwise, the voltage potential will differ throughout the system, defeating the original purpose of bonding the system.

Lightning Protection

Lightning strikes the planet a hundred times every second, with each strike at over a billion volts, over 100,000 amps, and with temperatures up to 30,000 °C. Lightning may not be a major concern in all regions, but if there is a lightning storm even a few times a year, consider using lightning protection devices. While not designed to stop lightning from striking, these devices encourage it to travel through a predetermined path in order to minimize the damage. No system is completely protected from lightning damage, but the right devices can decrease the chances of lightning causing any significant harm.

The first step in protecting from lightning is to have an appropriately grounded PV racking and electrical system. A robust grounding system will discharge accumulated static electricity and prevent the attraction of lightning. The fuses and breakers in your system provide no protection from lightning, because they are not designed for lightning protection and cannot blow or trip fast enough. But all of the electrically conductive components need to be bonded, and all of the electrical pathways need to share a grounding path. It is generally advisable to have only one grounding rod, because multiple rods would provide multiple paths for residual voltage after a lightning strike to travel.

Grounding rods need to be driven underground to 2.5 m at a minimum. If not, a grounding ring or buried conductor must be used to sufficiently provide a low-resistant path to ground. Ground rods will need more surface area in the earth in dry climates due to excess resistance, so they will need to be installed deeper than in wet climates.

If you determine that lightning protection is required for your system, then you will need to install **Surge Arrestors** and/or **Surge Capacitors**. These devices absorb electrical surges from lightning. (Of course, they can't protect your equipment unless the entire system is properly grounded.)

Surge arrestors clamp onto a wire with a parallel connection to the ground. If lightning strikes the wire, the giant electrical surge will jump to the surge arrestor clamp and prefer the path through the arrestor to ground. A Surge Capacitor can also provide protection but acts significantly faster than an arrestor.

Lightning damage is more common when a PV array or generator is located far away from the rest of the electrical system, as the long path of conductors might become a path for the lightning. Therefore, with any runs over 40 meters, use an arrestor on both sides. Use a DC surge arrestor on the PV input close to the charge controller. An AC surge arrestor should be added to protect the inverter as well. If using a generator, it's advisable to install both an AC surge arrestor and a surge capacitor.

In locations with frequent lightning strikes, lightning rods can dissipate the static charge down to the ground. They can help prevent a strike and also provide an alternate path to ground.

PV Mounting Selection

Before choosing your PV mounting system, be sure that it is designed for your wind and snow loads. If you have significantly high wind or snow loads, you might need to reinforce the racking system for increased strength. This could be done by reducing the length of the spans between beams, reducing cantilever lengths, and using deeper footings for a ground mount or more fastener attachments for a roof mount. If you are unsure and do not want to spend the time making the calculations, choose to over-build the system or hire a structural engineer licensed to practice in your locality. PV mounting materials can be inexpensive in the scope of the whole project.

Additionally, be sure that your PV mounting system is designed for the level of corrosion in your area. Highly corrosive environments include marine, coastal, and humid climates as well as areas with significant industrial processes, like a location near a factory. If you are in a corrosive environment, be sure to use all aluminum and stainless steel components. Ensure that components with mild steel have a thick enough galvanized coating to last at least 25 years. Basic pregalvanization coatings or paint might not last long enough in your area. If any parts of the galvanized steel are cut, then be sure to spray the ends with a galvanizing compound. Since hardware is so small and sensitive to corrosion, you should source stainless steel whenever possible.

Racking Types

Ground-Mounted PV Arrays

PV arrays can be mounted on a structure, like a rooftop, or mounted on a rack attached to the ground. Ideally arrays should be installed in a place with adequate protection and maximum solar access. The rooftop might be the first place you'd think to place the solar panels, but for off grid systems there is often open land available for a pole- or ground-mounted system.

As long as there is sufficient space, ground-mounted systems have many advantages over a roof mount. Ground mounts do not require climbing or safety ropes for the installation and do not require moving heavy equipment up and down ladders. Also, rooftop systems can have issues with roof leaks from penetrating the roofing membrane. Ground mounts typically have more airflow underneath, so the modules can operate at lower temperatures, which yields better performance. Ground mounts also allow for almost any tilt and azimuth angle, and can be designed to be adjustable for improved annual performance. Finally, having the modules closer to the ground allows for easier access for cleaning and reduced wind speeds.

There are a variety of ways to anchor a ground-mounted racking system, such as formed concrete piers, ballasted mounts (no ground penetration required), driven steel piles of beams or pipe, and earth screws (helical piers). With all of these options, the most common for a small- to medium-sized off grid system is a concrete pad or pier to form the base structure to which the base racking components will be attached.

For a pole-mounted system, consider a deep concrete pier, similar to the approach for a concrete fence post. Follow the directions for mixing concrete, as having too much or too little water can reduce the strength. Digging a hole and setting the concrete in the ground adds additional strength from friction of the ground around the footing. With above-ground concrete piers, more concrete is needed for the same amount of resistance to overturning.

TOP OF POLE-MOUNTED PV ARRAY

For larger racked systems, you will need to pour a concrete foundation with rebar reinforcement. These pads can run north to south and do not need to be deep. You can even use a concrete form and do this above ground, something like a ballasted system but poured in place.

Roof-Mounted PV Arrays

When there is no space or significant shading issues on the ground, then rooftop mounting has its own set of advantages worth considering. If the electricity will only be used in your home and batteries will be stored there as well, then a rooftop solar array might be best. That keeps the array close to where the energy is stored and consumed, allowing for shorter wire runs and less production loss from resistance. Also, the racking cost is generally cheaper for rooftop racking systems.

If your roof is flat, then the racking will need to tilt the modules up to a minimum of 5 degrees, but if the roof already has a tilt, verify it is appropriate for the energy production requirements of the system. All small rooftop PV systems need a mechanical attachment to the roof surface, which means you will have to put holes in the roof. If done incorrectly, the roof membrane penetration can become a pathway for water to enter your roof and damage your structure. Water damage would then occur very slowly, even if you don't notice a leak for years. Follow the racking manufacturer's instruction on how to seal the roof to ensure long-term reliability.

A typical rooftop mounting system has a post attachment with a long lag bolt that will attach to a rafter or purlin under the roof deck. Attaching to the roof deck only is not advised. Installing flashing and appropriate sealant over the post attachment is required to reduce the chance of a leak. Next, rails are attached to the post attachment, which creates a contiguous mounting plane where modules can be attached with room for adjustability. Finally, module clamps are used to secure the modules to the rail. See the diagram for details. On a flat roof, the post attachments will need to be different lengths to enable the PV array to be tilted.

The section view below is a common roofing design in North America for residential homes. It is typically a wood frame construction where the rafters are spaced apart at 16 inches (406mm) on center. Because the rafters are under the roof deck you need to find them to attach your lag bolts. Once you find one rafter you can usually measure over every 16 inches to find the next.

SECTION VIEW OF PV ARRAY ON PITCHED ROOF RAFTERS

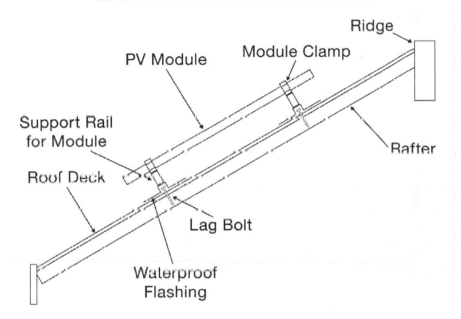

Another roofing design uses trusses. The section view below is more common in developing countries or for larger structures. It is typically a wood or steel frame where the trusses are further apart (usually 3-4 feet or 1 meter) than rafters are in the above example. The roof deck could be corrugated steel or plywood. With a truss design, there are fewer locations to fasten the support post attachment which can create challenges for the PV module arrangement. Be sure to evaluate the roofing dimensions and design your PV array attachment locations beforehand.

SECTION VIEW OF PV ARRAY ON PITCHED ROOF TRUSS

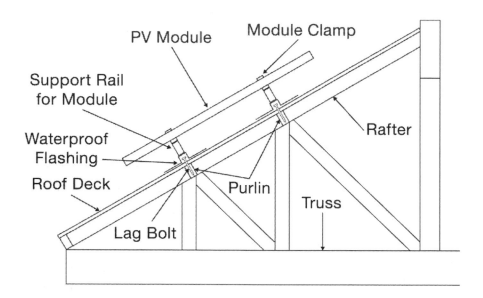

Adjustable Racking

With off grid PV systems, designing a racking system that can be adjusted to improve production is wise. Since it is best for solar power to be directly consumed when it is produced, try to aim the PV array to the optimal orientation. Tracking the sun may increase production as much as 5-30%! The sun is a moving target, however, and you might not actually need extra energy, so maximizing production isn't always necessary. This is only useful if your load profile can benefit from the additional energy. Adjustable racking can save the batteries when you need to maximize your energy production during cloudy days and winter months.

Adjustable racking can change the azimuth angle, the tilt angle, or both. Adjusting only the tilt angle increases performance on a seasonal basis. Manually adjusting the tilt angle once every 3-6 months is very practical and requires little effort on the part of the user. On the other hand, adjusting the azimuth angle manually on a daily basis is impractical.

The most complex tracking systems have motors with single-axis or dual-axis capabilities. These are relatively expensive and I would not recommend one unless you have a large PV array (over 30 kW). The simplest types of motorized tracking systems rotate the array around the axis perpendicular to the ground. (Picture a pole-mounted array that rotates around the vertical pole to give yourself an idea.) A motorized tracker like this could be useful in a smaller off grid PV system.

Passive Trackers are another option for tracking the sun. They do not require motors or electricity to orient the PV modules and can be more practical than the motorized trackers for smaller systems. Passive trackers have a chamber of liquid on each side of the array. If one chamber on the side gets hotter than the other, the liquid evaporates and shifts the weight of the tracker over to the other side, rotating the array toward the sun in the process. There are some limitations, though. For example, it can take more time for the array to "wake up" during the colder winter months. Also, the array will end each day pointed west, but to wake up in the morning it needs to shift the full distance to the east. Passive trackers are a good option for pole-mounted PV systems of small or medium size, but may not be cost effective for small systems with just a few PV modules. The image of the Top of Pole-Mounted PV Array a few pages back is an example of a passive tracker. Also, see the image on the next page.

PASSIVE TRACKER

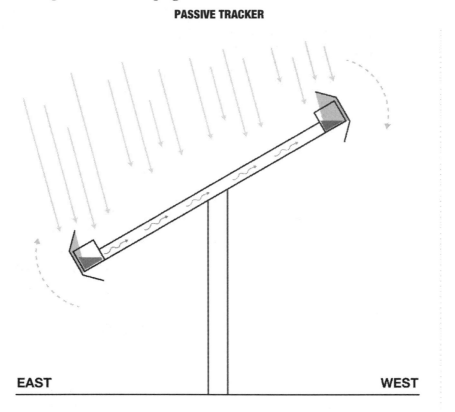

EAST   WEST

Finally, if you want to keep your system simple but still have some options for tilt adjustment, there are manually adjustable tilt-racking systems for pole-mounted or for racked systems. Manually adjusting the tilt angle or the azimuth occasionally can help if your load profile changes over the course of a season. Every system is different, but there is generally a latch that you'd pull in order to snap it into other positions. Some adjustable tilt racks use a cordless drill to rotate the rack and adjust the tilt angle. By adjusting only the tilt angle of a PV array, you should expect up to a 5-7% increase in performance.

Over the past decade the cost of solar has dropped significantly and it has made the additional cost of tracker systems less cost-effective. Be sure to evaluate system cost savings against the additional racking cost and maintenance required.

Mounting the Modules

The most common way to mount PV modules is with module clamps securing the module frame to the rail below. The clamps are tightened onto a steel or aluminum rail and are adjustable along the length of the rail. The adjustability is great in case all the parts do not match up perfectly. Module frames come in different sizes, so not all clamps work for all module types. Some clamps have teeth that will cut through the anodized layer on the module frame grounding it to the racking system. This is helpful because it grounds the system together when you tighten down the clamps.

PV Modules also have mounting holes on the back of the frame, which you can use to attach it to brackets or mounting rails. Different manufacturers may put mounting holes in the different places, so make sure the modules are compatible with the racking system before buying. Module clamps only work from the top of the module, so mounting holes are a better option when you want to attach the modules from under the racking system.

Hardware Considerations

Thread galling (also known as cold welding) may occur if using all stainless steel hardware for corrosion protection and fastening with an electric drill. This will result in nuts and bolts seizing, such that it is impossible to tighten or loosen them. This happens when two similar metals are in high-pressure or high-heat conditions and the sliding surfaces adhere to each other. If this happens during your installation your only option is to get a hacksaw and cut the fastener off and replace with a new one. To prevent your hardware from galling you can either use different alloys for the screws and nuts or you can use some "anti-seize" lubrication on the screws before you tighten the nuts.

If security is a concern, consider using tamper-proof hardware that requires special tool bits to tighten hardware so that it is very challenging to remove. I have seen circumstances where people use cement to secure the PV modules in place. I do not recommend doing this because submerging the PV module's aluminum frames in concrete can cause the aluminum to corrode.

Due to thermal cycling between hot and cold temperatures, hardware may loosen over time. This is a surprisingly common problem with custom built racking, especially if unsuitable hardware is used. Consider using flanged lock nuts, lock washers, or bonding adhesive for threads.

Wire Management

Addressing dangling wires under the solar panels can often be neglected until the very end of a project. When buying the racking system, also purchase wire clips that attach to the module frame or the racking equipment. The wire clips will hold the wires under the solar panels, hiding them from the sun and from view. Many people will use zip ties, which are better than nothing, but most zip ties will break within a few years from sun and weather exposure. If you must use zip ties, then select the thickest ones you can find with a UV inhibitor and use a lot of them in case some break early.

Whether attaching the wires with zip ties or with wire clips, always secure the wires so they won't come into contact with sharp edges. The mounting components and the wires will expand and contract from thermal cycling, so it may be imperceptible, but it is happening. If the wires are tight against a sharp edge, then the insulation may eventually tear, exposing the conductor to the racking system and ending in a short circuit or fire.

If you are using a tracking system or an adjustable racking system, be sure that the wiring will not break from the back and forth movement and fatigue. Also, be careful that this cyclical movement will not slowly pull the wire from its connections. Using strain reliefs will help if this occurs, but the wiring should be attached so it does not creep along the wire management edge.

Electrical Enclosure Selection

All of your system's electrical components need to be
protected from foreign objects (such as dirt and pests), rain,
condensation and other naturally occurring hazards that can
cause a short circuit or increase corrosion. The enclosure you
choose should have features that suit the conditions in which
it will be used. Will it be indoors or outdoors? Will it be
exposed to storms or humidity? Addressing any potential
problems prior to operation will help prevent them from
happening, or at least minimize any damage. Keeping water
out of electrical equipment ranks as the foremost priority for
the enclosure and can be quite challenging.

Water can enter into an enclosure in two ways: from rain
finding a way through a leak or from humidity condensing
inside the large, cooler interior of an enclosure. If water
ingress is a possibility, particularly in humid locations, then
drill a 6 mm "weep" hole on the bottom to allow built-up
water to exit. Any and all outdoor equipment will require
waterproof conductors, watertight wire connectors, and
watertight cord grips for the entry points into enclosures.

Be sure to purchase equipment with the appropriate
environmental rating. Otherwise, you may have to install your
equipment inside of a larger enclosure. This is both expensive
and adds potentially new problems. For example, let's say that
you purchase an indoor rated inverter and place it inside of an
outdoor rated enclosure, in a sunny location that will get very

hot. Because the enclosure is relatively small and has very little air movement, this may cause the inverter to overheat and malfunction. It would have been better to buy an outdoor rated inverter, so that it can ventilate the heat away from the electronics.

Ingress Protection

The **IP Code, International Protection Marking**, sometimes interpreted as **Ingress Protection Marking** (IEC standard 60529), classifies and rates the degree of protection provided against intrusion (body parts such as hands and fingers), dust, accidental contact, and water by mechanical casings and electrical enclosures. Typically an enclosure or piece of equipment will have an IP Code or IP Rating.

The IP Code has two numerical digits. The first digit indicates the level of protection that the enclosure provides against access to hazardous parts such as electrical conductors, moving parts, and the ingress of solid foreign objects such as fingers. The second digit indicates the level of protection that the enclosure provides against ingress of water. As the numbers increase in the IP Code, they also increase in the level of protection.

For example, an indoor electrical outlet with a rating of IP22 protects against shock by inserting your finger (first digit) and from becoming unsafe from vertically dripping water (second digit). But a cell phone with an IP rating of IP68 is dust resistant and can be immersed in 1.5 meters of fresh water for up to 30 minutes. See the table below for a more detailed description of the IP Code specifications.

IP CODE DEFINED

Level sized	First digit: Solid particle protection, Effective against	Second digit: Liquid ingress protection, Protection against
X	There is no data available to specify a protection rating with regard to these criteria.	There is no data available to specify a protection rating with regard to these criteria.
0	No protection against contact and ingress of objects	None
1	>50 mm	Dripping water
2	>12.5 mm	Dripping water when tilted at 15°
3	>2.5 mm	Spraying water
4	>1 mm	Splashing of water
5	Dust protected	Water jets
6	Dust tight	Powerful water jets
6K		Powerful water jets with increased pressure
7		Immersion, up to 1 m depth
8		Immersion, 1 m or more depth

The IP Rating is an internationally-recognized code, and if a product has a rating that means it has been tested to meet these standards. The IP rating is very similar to another standard for enclosures used in North America called NEMA.

NEMA Enclosure Types

The National Electrical Manufacturers Association (NEMA) defines enclosure types based on their use, and there are three types that are commonly used for solar projects. **NEMA Type 1** is designed for indoor use only and provides the most basic protection. **NEMA Type 3R** is designed for outdoor use and is good at protecting from storms and foreign objects while still allowing for ventilation. Because of its ventilation, it does not keep out humidity. **NEMA Type 4X** is also designed for outdoor use, but provides better protection from humidity since it is sealed.

If you are using lead-acid batteries, do not seal them inside a NEMA 4X enclosure. They will not be adequately ventilated, possibly trapping explosive gases and causing a dangerous situation. There are some enclosures designed so that the electronics are in a NEMA 4X section and the batteries are in a NEMA 3R section of the same enclosure. This is a good option if you want to buy just one enclosure for all your electronics and batteries.

The following definitions from NEMA 250-2003 are based on the use of the enclosure:

- **NEMA Type 1**: Enclosures constructed for indoor use to provide a degree of protection to personnel against access to hazardous parts and to provide a degree of protection of the equipment inside the enclosure against ingress of solid foreign objects (falling dirt).
- **NEMA Type 3R**: Enclosures constructed for either indoor or outdoor use to provide a degree of protection to personnel against access to hazardous parts; to provide a degree of protection of the equipment inside the enclosure against ingress of solid foreign objects (falling dirt); to provide a degree of protection with respect to harmful effects on the equipment due to the ingress of water (rain, sleet, snow); and that will be undamaged by the external formation of ice on the enclosure.
- **NEMA Type 4X**: Enclosures constructed for either indoor or outdoor use to provide a degree of protection to personnel against access to hazardous parts; to provide a degree of protection of the equipment inside the enclosure against ingress of solid foreign objects

(windblown dust); to provide a degree of protection with respect to harmful effects on the equipment due to the ingress of water (rain, sleet, snow, splashing water, and hose directed water); that provides an additional level of protection against corrosion; and that will be undamaged by the external formation of ice on the enclosure.

NEMA Rating and IP Code are different ratings but have similarities. Below is a table that shows how they compare.

NEMA COMPARED TO IP CODE

NEMA Enclosure	IP Code
1	IP20
2	IP22
3R	IP24
4X	IP66
6P	IP68

Low Cost Enclosures

For any PV system over 250 watts, I recommend corrosion-resistant sheet metal enclosures, preferably the NEMA-approved enclosures listed above. They can be expensive, but they will protect the most sensitive equipment in your PV system.

If you are designing a smaller system, consider repurposing a plastic case like a toolbox. Circular saws cut round holes for nylon cord grips and vents for airflow. Wooden enclosures are not recommended, since they will likely not keep out moisture or last as long. Regardless, they lack the convenience of a plastic toolbox.

Secondary Power Selection

Off grid solar systems can be very reliable most of the time, but there is always a possibility that the sun doesn't shine. Designing your system to function 100% of the time can be impractical for some situations, particularly in areas that have long, dark winters. The best solution for those types of sites is to include a secondary power source, such as a generator, wind power, or hydropower.

Generator

Despite the high cost of fuel from continued use, the high power output of generators can be quite helpful. This is particularly true during winter months, when generators can assist the PV array in charging your batteries. If you have a generator available to recharge batteries during cloudy days, you can reduce your days of autonomy, reducing your battery and PV size requirements significantly.

Generators can also prove useful if you plan to occasionally operate high-power equipment, such as power tools or heavy machinery, which might only be needed for an hour or two per month. In this circumstance the overall energy usage is low, but the instantaneous power usage is very high. Generators are very advantageous for just this type of situation, thanks to their high power output.

If you already have a generator, it might be challenging to integrate it correctly with your new battery system. You can manually charge the batteries with a separate AC-to-DC battery charger when possible. Or, if the battery levels drop too low and the inverter's LVD disconnects the load from the batteries, then you can manually start the old generator to power your equipment. Do not fully charge batteries with a generator; it can harm the batteries since they are designed to only be charged with the solar PV.

Automatic Transfer Switch (ATS)

Manually charging the batteries with a generator can be challenging, so I recommend designing a system where the generator automatically starts when the batteries drop below a certain voltage. To do this you will need an **Automatic Transfer Switch (ATS)** or an **Automated Generator Start (AGS)**, which can communicate with the battery inverter/charger and flip a relay switch to turn on the generator with an automatic starter. Starting a generator usually requires multiple stages to preheat and crank it on. The ATS or AGS should be customizable to match the needs of your particular generator. Sometimes the AGS will require a run signal from the generator in order to keep the generator charging the battery bank.

If you plan to buy a new generator with your off grid system, make sure the generator and the inverter are compatible. You need to get an inverter that communicates properly with an ATS or that has an AGS accessory, so it can automatically trigger the generator when the battery's SOC is low. Some inverters will have an auxiliary AC battery charger that is programmable with relay circuits to automatically trigger a generator when battery voltages are low.

Wind and Hydroelectric Power

Solar is an extraordinary off grid energy source, but under some circumstances and in certain locations, both wind and hydroelectric power can be fantastic alternatives. As with a generator an additional power source helps off grid solar systems when the winter days are not providing enough power to recharge the batteries. Wind and hydroelectric power are not as controllable as a generator, but you could potentially reduce the days of autonomy by one or two, allowing for a smaller battery bank and PV array. Fortunately, wind tends to blow both during the nighttime and wintertime and, in many regions, water flow peaks in the winter months. These are both opportunities to produce renewable power when solar energy is less abundant.

Exploring the benefits and requirements for these types of energy systems would fill an entire book in its own right. If you have access to other energy sources, be sure to properly understand how they can recharge your batteries or directly power your equipment. There are some charge controllers and inverters that are compatible with wind and hydro power, so if you plan to have a hybrid off grid system, be sure to research what equipment will work with all of your power generation sources.

Code Compliance

Before you begin designing your system, you need to confirm that it meets the local building code, which ensures that it will not be a safety hazard. You also need to confirm compliance with the local electrical code.

If you disregard local building and electrical codes, it can void the property insurance and cause problems when selling the property if the system is not compliant. Particularly in an urban area, it is advisable to hire an Electrical Engineer or certified solar installer to ensure your system is compliant, and most importantly, safe!

Following local building and electrical code has additional advantages. There are usually reference documents that walk you through the calculations and process to determine whether your system will pass inspection. Rather than guessing about what is important, these code requirements can guide you to make the right decisions.

Electrical Code Compliance

The **NFPA 70: *National Electrical Code*** (**NEC**) is a code standard for safe installation of electrical wiring and equipment in the United States. It has also been adopted as the national code in Mexico, Costa Rica, Venezuela and Colombia. The 2017 edition of *NFPA 70: National Electrical Code* has a whole new section about solar photovoltaic installations with new requirements, such as a rapid shutdown disconnect near the solar PV array.

The **International Electrotechnical Commission** IEC 60364 is used as a basis for electrical codes in many European countries. In Australia and New Zealand the **AS/NZS 3000:2018,** Electrical Installations, known as the Wiring Rules, are the technical rules that help electricians design, construct and verify electrical installations. It is recommended that you get familiar with the local electrical code or the code that is closest to where your will install your system.

Most electrical code compliance is designed to make your system safe, and focuses on preventing short circuits, ground faults, arc flashes, electrical fires, and other unsafe and undesirable outcomes. The code requires multiple means of disconnecting the system during an emergency. For example, if your house is on fire the fire department will usually go to the main panel and disconnect the main electricity panel, including your solar PV and battery system.

Professional electrical engineers and certified solar installers are familiar with code compliance because they are trained, experienced, and are liable when a local auditor visits the system and verifies its code compliance. If you chose to build your system without a professional, be sure to familiarize yourself and follow the local code. Figure out what electrical code has jurisdiction in your area and buy the code book or borrow it from your local library. I guarantee that reading through the code book and following the code compliance will be an educational, worthwhile experience that will make your system more reliable and improve your skill set.

Building Code Compliance

Many natural events can damage a system or create dangerous conditions, including wind, snow, seismic activity (earthquake), corrosion, or some combination of these factors. In the USA, states and localities model their building codes off of the International Building Code (IBC). For more detail on the design of your structure, consult the American Society of Civil Engineers (ASCE) code.

The ASCE publishes a manual that defines the minimum design requirements for structures. *"Minimum Design Loads for Buildings and Other Structures, ASCE/SEI 7-10, provides requirements for general structural design and includes means for determining dead, live, soil, flood, snow, rain, atmospheric ice, earthquake, and wind loads, as well as their combinations, which are suitable for inclusion in building codes and other documents."*

Depending on the material you are using for construction such as concrete, steel, or wood, there is a material code containing specifications, requirements and design calculations to help you select proper materials and sizing. As always, consult a licensed structural engineer where required by law, and if unsure.

Outside the US, most countries have local codes, many of which may base requirements on an international code or one from a neighboring place such as the US, Great Britain or Europe. If no building codes are available in your area, then the International Building Code (IBC) may be the most appropriate code to follow. Be sure to follow your local codes to ensure your system is safely installed and can withstand local weather conditions.

Wind Loads

The wind speeds and gust patterns for your area may seem small on a day-to-day basis, but you need to design the system for the worst conditions over its lifetime. Extreme weather may be inherently rare, but it is also inevitable. If the system will function for 30 years, it's a sure bet that it will experience wind loads much higher than expected. A large wind gust only needs to happen once to destroy your system.

A solar module with an area of 1.6 m² (17.2 ft²) in a high-wind location can experience loads as heavy as 350 kg-f (772 lbs). With four modules attached to a pole-mounted structure, the foundation could have an uplift force of 1400 kg-f (3088 lbs)! You will need to build a foundation and racking system that will not break or buckle from these load conditions for upward, downward, and lateral forces. If you are unsure about how strong your structure should be, it is best to overbuild the system to be stronger than necessary — better yet, consult a licensed structural engineer!

Snow Loads

Snow build-up can cause solar structures to collapse—not only from the dead weight of the snow, but from the snow's weight as it slides off the edge, redistributing the center of gravity on top of the solar panels. Reducing the cantilever and distance between spans on the racking system will help ensure this doesn't happen. Snow loads can be particularly problematic for pole-mounted racking because the pole-mounted structure needs to be strong enough to resist bending caused by eccentric force due to the sliding snow.

Seismic (Earthquake) Loads

Earthquakes can affect the structure in unpredictable ways. An earthquake may not shake the structure enough to break the solar modules from the racking, but it might cause the electrical wiring to tear away from the system. This can lead to a short circuit or ground fault that could very easily turn into a fire. Be sure to run electrical wiring through a flexible conduit between structures that can move.

Corrosion

Corrosion can vary greatly, depending on location of the install. Near the ocean, salt in the air can cause metal to rust and dissolve. This compromises the strength of the structure and could rust the hardware, making it impossible to remove for maintenance. Pollution from a nearby factory or industrial area can also create corrosive conditions.

Don't let a racking supplier fool you! You might need to buy more expensive racking to withstand your particular environment. It might even be necessary to use all aluminum or stainless steel components in highly corrosive environments. But when corrosion risk is low, steel with a galvanized coating or paint can function just as well.

Determine the corrosivity of the site location and design the system appropriately. On the next page is a table from the International Organization for Standardization (ISO) that determines the corrosivity category and risk. The thickness loss values are after the first year of exposure. Losses may reduce over subsequent years.

For coastal areas in hot, humid zones, the mass or thickness losses can exceed the limits of category C5-M. Special precautions must therefore be taken when selecting protective paint systems for structures in those areas.

ATMOSPHERIC CORROSIVITY CATEGORIES AND EXAMPLES OF TYPICAL ENVIRONMENTS (BS EN ISO 12944-2)

Corrosivity category and risk	Low-carbon steel Thickness loss (µm)	Examples of typical environments in a temperate climate (informative only)	
		Exterior	Interior
C1 very low	≤ 1.3	-	Heated buildings with clean atmospheres, e.g. offices, shops, schools, hotels
C2 low	> 1.3 to 25	Atmospheres with low level of pollution Mostly rural areas	Unheated buildings where condensation may occur, e.g. depots, sports halls
C3 medium	> 25 to 50	Urban and industrial atmospheres, moderate sulfur dioxide pollution Coastal area with low salinity	Production rooms with high humidity and some air pollution e.g. food-processing plants, laundries, breweries, dairies
C4 high	> 50 to 80	Industrial areas and coastal areas with moderate salinity	Chemical plants, swimming pools, coastal, ship and boatyards
C5-I very high (industrial)	> 80 to 200	Industrial areas with high humidity and aggressive atmosphere	Buildings or areas with almost permanent condensation and high pollution
C5-M very high (marine)	> 80 to 200	Coastal and offshore areas with high salinity	Buildings or areas with almost permanent condensation and high pollution

Pests or Animals

Pests pose their own set of risks to solar energy systems. The most common problems come from bird droppings shading the PV modules, or rodents crawling under the modules to chew on wires. Falling leaves or debris collecting near chewed wires can cause fires. Consider caging off the edge of rooftop PV arrays if there are concerns about rodents and falling leaves.

Don't underestimate the power of nature to destroy an off grid solar energy system. I've heard stories where goats were used to eat overgrown brush near solar arrays, only to damage modules by jumping on top of them. I even heard an instance of elephants that wandered over to a PV array thinking it was a pond, but after realizing it was not water, they sat on it out of disappointment. When you are designing your system, do your best to research what sort of risks the local wildlife might pose.

System Design

Generation Capacity vs. Storage Capacity

If you increase your battery capacity do you also need to increase your solar system size? If you use most of your loads at night and nothing during the day, do you need more or fewer batteries? The balance between solar production and battery storage can be challenging to dial in just right. You want to minimize cost but also ensure your batteries always get fully charged. Both generation capacity and storage capacity need to be appropriate for the size of the load.

If the generation capacity (solar production) is too low compared to the storage capacity, then the batteries will never get fully charged and will fail much sooner than expected. You need to make sure that the PV modules produce power for long enough hours to fully charge the batteries under normal use in the winter. If the PV does not completely recharge the batteries a few days a year, that's OK, but not for weeks at a time.

When the majority of your energy loads occur during the day, you might have more solar and fewer batteries compared to a system with higher loads in the evenings. That's because you can use the solar energy during the day as it is being produced, thereby skipping the batteries.

If you have too much generation capacity compared to storage capacity, then all you have is extra unused solar energy. No harm done! … other than spending too much money on solar panels. Cost aside, be sure you are determining the worst-case scenario during a cloudy day in winter, because you want to make sure your batteries always charge fully no matter the season or weather.

It is very common for an off grid system to have unused solar energy in the summer. In those cases where your batteries are full and you have no other loads, consider using a diversion load (dump load), because otherwise that energy will be lost forever. You can divert unusable energy to a fan, air conditioner, hot water heater, or ice machine. The summer heat is plentiful so you might as well put that free extra power to work for you.

System Sizing

As noted in the *Site Design* chapter, you should have determined energy needs as well as essential power needs, daily energy requirements, and local solar irradiation. In the equipment selection chapters, you should have determined the best combination of equipment for your system. This chapter is about how to identify and balance battery and solar requirements.

Once you know your equipment needs, you're ready to get quotes from contractors to install the system for you. But there is more work to be done if you want to install the system yourself. You will need to find out what equipment is locally available and begin to design accordingly. For example, don't design your system around particular battery specifications if those are not readily available near you.

To properly engineer the system, first determine your system requirements, get a quote, and finally create a bill of materials and line diagrams to ensure the system is designed correctly.

Visit the link below to download the *System Designer* spreadsheet. It has a load calculation table, derate table, and all the calculations used in this chapter.

www.OffGridSolarBook.com/Resources

Battery System Voltage

In an off grid solar energy system you need to determine an appropriate **Battery System Voltage,** or the nominal operating voltage for the battery bank and charge controller.

For lead-acid batteries, you should have a voltage of 12, 24, 36, or 48 volts. It is common to have an off grid solar system at 12 Vdc for systems up to 1000 watts, 24 Vdc for systems around 2000 watts, and 48 Vdc for systems above 5000 watts. Using numerous low-voltage batteries in series is better than using many high-voltage batteries in parallel. A string of low-voltage batteries in series act like one giant battery. Also, avoid more than 3 strings of batteries in parallel.

Lithium-ion batteries can use a substantially higher voltage, because the BMS is designed to make it safer for the user. Smaller systems frequently use 12-48 Vdc, but lithium-ion manufacturers are starting to support higher voltage systems with the BMS functions at 400 Vdc. The lithium-ion battery industry is undergoing a lot of change now, and each manufacturer is following their own standards. In the future, there will probably emerge a common practice for battery system voltage, likely to settle around 380-400 Vdc.

The lower the voltage, the safer the system is to install, but the higher the resistance on the electronics. With a higher battery voltage, the current will be lower relative to power, with less internal resistance, allowing the components to function at a lower temperature. This will extend their usable life. Remember, high current means more losses due to resistance—that's why higher current requires thicker wires.

Keep in mind that the solar voltage needs to exceed the battery system voltage by about 20% to account for losses. For example, if you have a 48 Vdc battery system and each PV module is 29 Vmp, then you should have strings of three PV modules to exceed the 48Vdc (assuming it is not exceeding the limits of the charge controller). Also, most charge controllers and inverters have a maximum current rating but a range of acceptable voltages, usually 12-24 Vdc or 12-48 Vdc. Designing for a higher voltage, therefore, will allow for a larger system size with the same equipment.

Derate Factor

Every single piece of equipment in your solar energy system has inefficiencies, from the solar cell to the electrical socket powering the equipment. Each of the inefficiencies add up to a **Derate Factor**. There are losses from solar module tolerances and mismatches, soiling and shading on the solar modules, temperature effects on the PV cells, resistance in the wires, battery inefficiencies, charge controller and inverter inefficiencies, just to name a few.

DERATE FACTOR LIST

Component Derate Factors	Range	Example
PV module nameplate DC rating	0.80 – 1.05	0.95
PV Temperature	0.85 – 1.05	0.95
Soiling	0.30 – 0.995	0.95
Mismatch	0.97 – 0.995	0.98
Diodes and connections	0.99 – 0.997	0.99
DC wiring	0.97 – 0.99	0.98
Charge Controller	0.88 – 0.98	0.95
Battery Round Trip Efficiency	0.80 – 0.98	0.85
Inverter	0.88 – 0.98	0.92
AC wiring	0.98 – 0.993	0.99
Shading	0.00 – 1.00	N/A
Sun-tracking	0.95 – 1.00	N/A
Age (~1% per year)	0.70 – 1.00	N/A
DC Derate Factor		**0.658**
AC Derate Factor		**0.911**
Overall Derate Factor		**0.600**

The list above shows an example of how the inefficiencies in a typical off grid solar energy system are significant and need to be accounted for in your calculations.

The DC Derate Factor takes into account everything from the PV array to the battery bank, and the AC Derate Factor takes into account everything after the battery bank. The Overall Derate Factor includes everything. These derate factors will be used in the next few calculations.

The derate factor for shading can have the largest impact on the solar production. Check to make sure that there is no shading between 9am and 3pm. If there is, reduce your shading derate appropriately. See The Effects of Module Shading in the Photovoltaic Module Selection chapter for more details. You can use a solar pathfinder and accurately calculate your shading derate factor. To learn more about solar pathfinder see the Tools section in this chapter.

Battery Sizing

The *Site Design* chapter addressed how to measure Daily Energy Usage with a Load Calculation Table. The **Daily Energy Requirement** is the demand on the battery for each day. To find it, account for the overall derate factor. This is also the amount of energy required from the PV array to fully recharge the battery bank. The example below expands on the Load Calculation Table in the *System Design* chapter with some more assumptions.

To find the Daily Energy Requirements:

$$\frac{Daily\ Energy\ Usage}{Overall\ Derate}$$

$$\frac{1470\ Wh}{0.60} = 2450\ Wh$$

Next, determine the **Battery Capacity** in amp-hours. This is the capacity of the battery bank based on the Daily Energy Requirements, the battery system voltage, the depth of discharge (DOD), and days of autonomy. Let's assume a 24-V Battery System Voltage and 3 days of autonomy. The DOD is based on battery type, so let's assume lead-acid batteries.

To find Battery Capacity:

$$\frac{Daily\ Energy\ Requirements}{Battery\ System\ Voltage} \div DOD \times Days\ of\ Autonomy$$

$$\frac{2450\ Wh}{24V} \div 0.5 \times 3 = 613\ Ah$$

For this example you will need a battery bank that totals 24 V and 613 Ah. There are a variety of ways to get the battery bank to this voltage and capacity by combining them in parallel and series strings. For example, one could use twelve 12-V, 105-Ah batteries in a configuration of six parallel strings of two in series. However, with this many parallel connections, the small variations in voltage between each string will stress the batteries and decrease their lifespan. To reduce this stress, limit the parallel connections by using lower-voltage batteries in series. A better set-up would be eight batteries of 6 V and 310 Ah in a configuration of two parallel strings of four in series.

In researching battery selection, base your calculations on the capacity at an appropriate discharge rate. Remember batteries have internal resistance and have a smaller capacity if discharged more quickly. For example, if a battery has a 310 Ah at a 24-hour rate (0.04 C) and a 280 Ah at an 8-hour rate (0.13 C), then this battery would be too small. If anticipated energy consumption is very regular and constant, then a 24-hour rating might make sense. That said, if you use more energy in the evenings, then an 8-hour rating would be a better choice.

It is also worth noting that if lithium-ion batteries were used in the example above, all variables would be approximately the same, except for the DOD. Typically, lithium-ion batteries use a 0.80 DOD, and in this case the battery capacity would be 383 Ah, requiring a smaller battery capacity compared to a lead-acid system.

Battery Current Requirements

Calculate the **Peak Discharge Current** by dividing the maximum Continuous Power rating on the inverter by the Battery System Voltage and then divide that by the AC Derate Factor. In this example, I am using an inverter with a maximum continuous power rating of 1000 watts.

To find the Peak Discharge Current:

$$\frac{Inverter\ Continuous\ Power}{Battery\ System\ Voltage} \div AC\ Derate$$

$$\frac{1000\ W}{24\ V} \div 0.911 = 45.7\ A$$

The Peak Discharge Current calculates the worst-case discharge on the battery bank. It shows that if the inverter is fully loaded, then the battery bank will discharge close to 50 A. You could also use the Peak Power to figure out the Peak Discharge Current if you plan to never use the full-power window on the inverter.

Using the Peak Discharge Current you can determine the **Peak Discharge Rate** on the batteries. Some batteries can be damaged if discharged too quickly, so this describes the worst-case rate of discharge on the battery bank.

To find the Peak Discharge Rate:

$$\frac{Battery\ Capacity}{Peak\ Discharge\ Current} = \frac{613\ Ah}{45.7\ A} = 13.4\ h$$

$$13.4\ h = 0.07C$$

If the battery capacity was 613 Ah, then discharging at maximum load on the inverter would take 13.4 hours, or a C-rate of 0.07 C. Under a normal load of 600 watts, that discharge rate drops to 22 hours or 0.04 C. I recommend discharging lead-acid batteries no faster than an 8-hour rate or 0.13 C. Some VRLA AGM batteries can discharge at a 4-hour rate or 0.25 C and lithium-ion batteries can discharge up to a 1-hour rate or 1 C.

PV Sizing

Now that you know the energy requirements and battery bank requirements, you need to size the PV array large enough to recharge the batteries under worst-case conditions, ensuring there is energy available on cloudy winter days.

The *System Design* chapter includes a section about Solar Insolation and Peak Sun Hours (PSH), describing how every location has a different level of solar energy available. In addition, there are larger seasonal variations at greater distances from the equator. In order to determine the correct number of solar panels for the system, assume the worst-case scenario and determine how much energy is available in the wintertime, or the winter PSH.

It can be challenging to determine the winter PSH, but entering your location into the NREL's PVWatts website (pvwatts.nrel.gov) will yield an approximation of local available energy. Find the lowest value out of all twelve months. For my example, I will build it in my backyard in Oakland, California. After entering the data on the PVWatts Calculator for my location, it shows a table of the Solar Radiation per Month. In December the Solar Radiation ($kWh/m^2/day$) is 2.88, the lowest of all the months. The solar radiation is equal to the PSH.

To find the **Minimum Solar Production**:

Daily Energy Requirements

Winter PSH

$$\frac{2450\ Wh}{2.88\ PSH} = 850.7\ watts$$

In other words, I need 851 watts of solar panels to fully recharge the batteries on an average Oakland day in December. Using four 250-watt PV modules would total 1000 watts and should be able to recharge the system even on the cloudiest winter days. Now we need to decide how we will wire the modules together. Should we go in series or parallel? If we use an MPPT Charge Controller, it has an advantage over PWMs in that it can handle a large PV open-circuit voltage.

In this example, I will use a 24 V, 40 A Max MPPT Charge Controller with a maximum input voltage of 120 Voc. A higher input voltage allows for more modules to be attached in series, which reduces the amount of wire needed to run to the controller and potentially eliminates the need for a combiner box.

In the *Equipment Selection* chapter, the section on Photovoltaics describes PV array maximum voltage for cold climates. Since the open-circuit voltage (Voc) may increase on cold days, ensure that the string of modules will not exceed the voltage limits of the rest of the system. In this example we need to determine the worst-case open-circuit voltage (Voc) of the string of modules. The temperature coefficient (TC_{Voc}) located on the PV module specification sheet is needed to determine the Voc for the site based on the lowest recorded temperature in Oakland, California.

First, find the lowest temperature on record for the site, not the lowest *average* temperature. In Oakland it is 1 °C. Next find the temperature coefficient (TC_{Voc}) on the PV module specification. For this module it is -0.34% per °C.

$$- 0.34\%/°C \times (25°C - (1°C)) = -7.2\%$$

$$37.2\,V \times (1 - (-7.2\%)) = 40.2\,V$$

The adjusted Voc for this PV module in Oakland is 40.2 V and the charge controller's maximum input voltage is 120 V. Divide the maximum inverter voltage input by the adjusted open-circuit voltage, yielding 2.9. This means that using three modules together in a string would potentially exceed the requirements of the charge controller, so we need to use two modules per string.

$$\frac{Max\ Inverter\ Input}{Adjusted\ Voc} = \frac{120\,V}{40.2\,V} = 2.9 = 2\ modules\ per\ string$$

This confirms that the maximum open-circuit voltage for two modules in series, even on the coldest day on record in Oakland, will not exceed the input voltage tolerance on the charge controller. Since we need four modules total, we will have two strings in parallel and each string will have two modules in series.

System Specifications

At this point you should have the specifications of all the major components in the system and should have already made sure that the components are appropriately balanced and compatible. You're now ready to get started on sourcing and pricing your system. Be careful, though: if you change one component, then you might need to go back and change everything else. For example, if you switch from using higher-wattage PV modules at the last minute, then you might need to change your charge controller too if the Voc is exceeded. This could set off a chain of events that would demand switching out extensive equipment to ensure it is all compatible.

Below is a list of the equipment specifications based on everything we've calculated so far. This list is what you will use to assemble a Bill of Materials and make line diagrams.

OFF GRID SOLAR

EXAMPLE SYSTEM SPECIFICATIONS

AC Load: 4 LED lights, 2 cell phone chargers, a fan, a LCD TV, and a water pump

Peak Continuous Power	600 W
Peak Surge Power	1600 W
Daily Energy Usage	1470 Wh

Battery: VRLA AGM

Nominal Voltage	6 V
Capacity @ 8-hour rate	310 Ah
Batteries in series	4
Serial strings in parallel	2
Total Capacity @ 8-hour rate	14.7 kWh

Charge Controller: MPPT

Battery System Voltage	24 V
Maximum Input Voltage	120 Voc
Maximum Current	40 A

Inverter: Pure Sine Wave

Max Continuous Power	1000 W
Max Surge Power	2000 W

PV Module: 60-cell, P-Si

Max Power (STC)	250 W
Open-circuit voltage, Voc	37.2 V
Maximum power point voltage, Vmp	30.1 V
Short-circuit current, Isc	8.87 A
Maximum power point current, Imp	8.3 A
Modules in series	2
Serial strings in parallel	2
Adjusted open-circuit voltage, Voc	80.5 V
Adjusted short-circuit current, Isc	17.5 A
Total PV Power (STC)	1000 W

Bill of Materials

It's not necessary to compile a **Bill of Materials** (BOM) until you are ready to purchase the equipment, but it can be helpful to have a preliminary BOM while designing the system. A preliminary BOM will start with just the major components, but as it is finalized, the BOM should also include the balance of system components and all of the other parts needed to completely install the system. The BOM should have at minimum: each item name, description, quantity, and cost. Other helpful categories are part number, source/store, and length (if purchasing wire per-length rather than per-quantity).

On the next page is a preliminary BOM based on the example so far. Templates are available on my website at the following link, under *Bill of Materials*.

www.OffGridSolarBook.com/Resources

EXAMPLE BILL OF MATERIALS

Description	QTY	Subtotal	Total
PV Module, Canadian Solar, 250W	4	$223	$892
Battery, Xtender, VRLA AGM, 6V nominal, 310Ah @ 8-hour rate	8	$414	$3,312
Charge Controller, Morningstar, MPPT, 24V, 40A max, 120Voc Input	1	$299	$299
Inverter, Samlex PST-1000, Pure Sine Wave, 1000w, 2000w surge	1	$349	$349
4-module top of pole, racking system	1	$595	$595
Electronics and Battery Enclosure, NEMA3R/4X	1	$445	$445
Load Center with breakers	1	$149	$149
PV disconnect with fuses	1	$64	$64
Battery disconnect with fuses	1	$84	$84
PV wire, 10AWG (per meter)	30	$1.47	$44
Battery wire, 2AWG, 2m, with crimped connectors	1	$65	$65
DC wire, 10AWG (per meter)	2	$6	$12
AC wire, Romex 14AWG (per meter)	80	$0.30	$24
Misc. Connectors, Hardware, etc...	1	$100	$100
TOTAL			**$6,434**

If you plan on getting quotes from installers, they will often send one with differing equipment specifications, making cost comparison difficult. Analyze the bids for cost per AC watt (including all the derate factors from inefficiencies). Next, analyze for the cost per kWh of batteries, and compare based on the same depth of discharge (DOD) at the same discharge rate (such as C/24).

Component Layout and Installation

Having sized all of the equipment in the system, you can evaluate how everything interconnects, and whether the system is balanced.

You should install the charge controller, inverter, and battery bank all within 2 meters of each other if possible; the closer the better. Also, plan to have them shaded and protected from the elements. If they must be outdoors, make sure they will not get wet and are protected in an appropriate enclosure. The batteries and electronics will last longer and be more efficient if they are in mild ambient temperatures, rarely getting too hot or cold. Keep in mind that any lead-acid batteries (including the sealed VRLA type) should not be located inside of a sealed enclosure because of escaping gas. The fuse or breaker on the battery bank needs to be extremely close to the positive terminal, usually within 25 cm.

Line Diagrams

Off grid energy systems require the interconnection of just a few components, but the diversity of all the circuits can get complicated quickly. There are AC and DC circuits with many junction points, disconnects, and overload protections connected to products from different manufacturers. The complexity comes from the multiple pathways the electricity can travel; line diagrams are a map of the circuit. There is no need to make the drawing to scale or to represent the actual size of the components, because mapping the conductor pathways and relationships between components is what's important.

Once you know which components you will use, sketch them on a piece of paper and draw a line connecting the inputs to the outputs. This is a **single line diagram**, which will help you determine the series and parallel connection points as well as how the wires will be distributed. With a single line, you can ignore the positive, negative, and grounding conductors and just acknowledge that the components have a closed pathway. Use this single line to explain to yourself and others what the plan is. Include notes about quantities, fuse sizes, distances, location, enclosure type, power requirements, etc.

EXAMPLE SINGLE LINE DRAWING

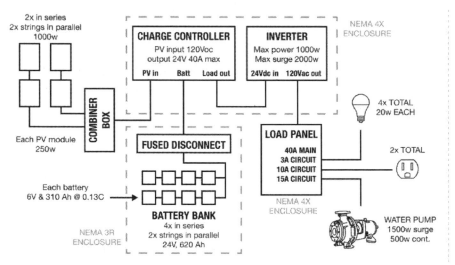

After creating a single line diagram, make a **three line** or multi-line diagram showing greater detail, including the positive, negative, and grounding paths with wire type and sizes, number of conductors, and the conduit type and size. Both types of line diagrams should show the connection path between the PV modules, charge controllers, inverters, batteries, combiner boxes, fuses/breakers, and disconnects. Once the line diagrams are complete, they can be compared to the BOM to determine if anything has been overlooked or forgotten.

You will be required to present a complete three-line diagram if submitting permits to a building department. Otherwise, not all projects require one, but it will certainly help during the design phase. Most importantly, a three-line diagram will help determine what's been forgotten, such as the type of conductors, connections, termination, and circuit protection.

Often, without a three-line diagram, small things get overlooked until the system is getting installed. If you don't have access to an electrician's equipment supply, then you might not be able to complete your installation. For example, when you plan to have multiple wires connect together in parallel, will you use DIN rail terminal blocks, wire connector nuts, or block connectors? Are you using compatible wire types and sizes to connect between your equipment? Line diagrams are great for project review and implementation, especially if installing in a remote location without extra supplies.

Installation Safety

CAUTION: Danger to life due to high voltage. Risk of death and serious injury due to electric shock.

I strongly encourage you to hire a licensed local electrician or a properly trained and qualified installer to complete the final connections and energize the system. Only work directly with the equipment if you have proper training.

This book does not cover proper electrician training. If you have experience with constructing electrical equipment, proceed with caution. Consider only working with low-voltage systems such as 12-volts, or never work with live equipment.

Personal Protective Equipment (PPE) is used during an installation to protect the installer and anyone else nearby. This includes hardhats, safety glasses, safety shoes, gloves, and fall protection equipment. All of this equipment may not be necessary in every case, but safety glasses, gloves, and closed-toed shoes are always an absolute must.

Always assume any circuit you are working on is live with electricity. Better safe than sorry! If you see any liquid near lead-acid batteries, always assume it is battery acid. Do not touch it! It will burn skin and clothes. Dab a cloth in a solution of baking soda mixed with water to clean off the top of the battery if necessary.

Tools

You may not need every one of these tools for every job, but I bring them to every installation just in case. You never want to be missing the right tool for the job.

Kill A Watt Meter

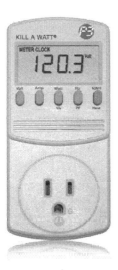

The Kill A Watt® meter plugs into a standard AC outlet and can measure kilowatt-hours (kWh), watts (W), volts (V), amps (A), line frequency (Hz), apparent power (VA), and power factor (PF). This meter only works on the AC side of your system after the inverter. If you want to measure anything on the DC side, you need a multimeter or clamp meter. The voltage and current are measured using the accurate RMS method and the meter has over current protection.

A Kill A Watt meter primarily measures the power of individual equipment and appliances, thus helping you determine your consumption per device for your load calculation table. It can also find out if you have voltage drop on any of the AC wiring throughout your system. When a significant drop in voltage is found (a drop of 10 volts or more between two parts of the same circuit), there is improper or malfunctioning wiring.

Multimeters

Multimeters get their name because they can measure multiple things, such as voltage, current, and resistance. They are a valuable troubleshooting tool, which can help diagnose many problems in your energy system.

The simplest function is to check for continuity, ensuring that sections of the circuit are as interconnected as intended. Check the resistance between two points in the circuit to determine if they are electrically connected.

Another easy and important function of a multimeter is to check the voltage. Testing the voltage is safe, because it does not interrupt the circuit, only measuring the voltage difference between two points. The larger the voltage, the more dangerous the test. Before touching any part of an electrical system, make sure to be properly equipped and educated.

Testing continuity and voltage is safe and easy, but testing current with the probes of a standard multimeter is not. Since this interrupts the circuit, electricity flows through the multimeter. Since there is little resistance in your new circuit, the current can be very high, causing a dangerous situation with the potential to blow the fuse in the multimeter. To test the current, do so with a clamp meter.

Clamp Meter

Clamp Meters, also known as Current Clamps, are multimeters equipped with a clamp to measure current indirectly. Measuring current is safer with a clamp because it does not interrupt the circuit for the measurement. Instead, a clamp meter analyzes the magnetic field in a conductor, without having to make physical contact with it or disconnect it. Clamp meters are effective at measuring currents over 1 ampere; anything lower than 1 A is difficult to measure accurately with a clamp meter.

There are some multimeters and clamp meters that have the capability to measure the inrush current of a circuit. This is particularly helpful for designing a system with large motors. Look for an "inrush" button to see if the clamp meter has this capability. Clamp meters cannot measure very quick pulses of current, but for the inrush on a motor it will give a reasonable approximation. To really understand quick inrush current, use an oscilloscope, but this is very impractical for most situations.

Angle Gauge / Angle Finder / Inclinometer

This tool determines the actual tilt angle of your solar array or the roof pitch. Some have a magnetic bottom that can be mounted to ferrous metals and tilted to the appropriate angle.

Magnetic Compass

A magnetic compass points to the magnetic north pole— but that may not always be true north for every location. You must take into account the declination of the area. Revisit Finding True North in the *System Design* chapter for more details.

Solar Pathfinder

A Solar Pathfinder measures the path of the sun and the shade from obstacles in a particular location. This helps determine what the actual PV production will be by accounting for the shade. This product is non-electronic, simple, and requires little skill to use properly. There are other electronic tools that are more complex but can digitize the results, such as the Solmetric Suneye.

Hydrometer

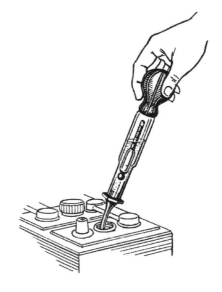

A hydrometer measures the specific gravity in flooded lead-acid batteries. By measuring the specific gravity in the batteries, you can more accurately determine the voltage of each cell and the batteries' health. If the voltage difference between cells is 0.2 V or more, it's time to perform an equalizing charge on the batteries. A large difference of voltage between cells is also a sign of a malfunctioning or dead battery, or possibly of sulfated cells.

Depending on the manufacturer and battery type, most flooded lead-acid batteries will read 2.12 to 2.15 VPC (Volts per Cell) at 100% charge, 2.03 VPC at 50% charge, and 1.75 VPC at 0% charge. The specific gravity will be 1.265 per cell at 100% charge and 1.13 or less for a completely discharged cell.

State of Charge, Specific Gravity and Open-Circuit Voltage

Approximate State of Charge	Average Specific Gravity at 26° C	Open circuit voltage			
		2V	6V	8V	12V
100%	1.265	2.1	6.32	8.43	12.65
75%	1.225	2.08	6.22	8. 30	12.45
50%	1.19	2.04	6.12	8.16	12.24
25%	1.155	2.01	6.03	8.04	12.06
0%	1.12	1.98	5.95	7.72	11.89

Correct the Specific Gravity readings to 26° C:
- Add .007 to readings for every 10° above 26° F
- Subtract .007 from reading for every 10° above 26° F

Portable WiFi GSM Modem

A GSM modem uses a cellular phone SIM card and operates with a mobile phone subscription. It creates a portable WiFi hotspot, and sometimes also has an Ethernet plug. This can be extremely useful for troubleshooting communication problems with inverters and for downloading firmware or updated instruction manuals.

Operations and Maintenance

Below is a checklist that will help identify possible problems that can come from age or the environment and will help ensure your system is functioning properly. It is important to carry out this entire checklist at least once a year, and some of the items should be completed even more frequently.

Battery Examination

- Inspect the area around the batteries for liquid that could turn out to be leaking battery acid. Use extreme caution with any liquid near batteries.
- Check to see if the sides of the battery cases are bloated. This is a sign of undercharging, over-discharging, and/or sulfate build-up. Follow equalizing procedure if bloated.
- Let the batteries rest without charge or discharge for at least 6 hours. Test the voltage between batteries and between battery cells (if possible) to ensure there are minimal voltage differences. Follow equalizing procedure if there is a significant difference in voltage.
- For flooded batteries, check the specific gravity with a hydrometer. Follow equalizing procedure if there is a significant difference in specific gravity between cells.

Inverter and Charge Controller Examination

- Cycle through the user interface if available and record the set points, voltages, and production values. Record the last logged error if available.
- Clean air filters and inside of the cabinet if accessible.
- Examine the fan and test for proper use.
- Check fuses, circuit breakers, and lightning arrestors near the equipment.
- Test for continuity on the system ground and equipment ground.

Racking System Examination

- Remove any vegetation that may have grown tall enough to shade the modules.
- Examine PV modules for defects such as discoloration, delamination, or broken glass.
- Check concrete footings and ground connections for erosion or damage. Look for signs of cracking or wear.
- Check racking for rust or corrosion, particularly on edges and on hardware.
- Check racking for sagging or broken parts, make sure cantilevered spans are not bowing or twisting.
- Check for signs of animal or pest infestation, such as nests, chewed wires, dislodged parts, etc.
- Make sure none of the wires are bent, discolored, or showing signs of wear. Determine the cause of loose, hanging wire and properly affix it back into place, avoiding sharp edges.

For rooftop arrays:
- Check integrity and watertight seal on rooftop penetrations.

- Check drainage on roof around racking equipment. Remove clogs or damming to prevent water pooling.

For trackers or adjustable racking:
- Check for signs of parts rubbing or hitting each other
- Lubricate gears with a grease per manufacturer recommendations.
- Recalibrate the position of the inclinometer with a digital level.

Battery Maintenance

The most important thing you can do to protect and extend the life of your off grid solar energy system is to care for your batteries. Lead-acid batteries can be irreparably damaged through misuse or neglect. Common problems with batteries are sulfate build-up, loss of electrolytes, and undercharging. Luckily, the charge controller and/or inverter will protect the batteries from the most common issues of over-charging or discharging. However, they will not protect the batteries from lack of charging in the first place. An energy source (like solar) must still push energy into the batteries. If necessary, consider getting a backup generator to charge the batteries in the winter months. See the Generator section in the *Secondary Power Selection* chapter for more details about using a generator with your off grid solar energy system.

When purchasing new lead-acid batteries, buy right before installation or make sure they don't sit longer than a week or two without a full charge. If buying them early, trickle charge before putting them in use. Brand new batteries will not reach their full capacity until they have been cycled up to 30 times. During the first few weeks of operation, a battery will likely function 5% to 10% lower than its rated capacity.

When purchasing new lithium batteries, it is recommended to read the manufacturer's manual for initial operation. They are often delivered at low SOC (~30%) due to dangerous goods delivery requirements, so you don't want them to sit unused for longer than a few months, nor in hot, humid environments.

Inverter and Charge Controller Maintenance

Most inverters and charge controllers are warrantied for 10 years, and usually only last about that long, eventually wearing out even if they are used according to the manufacturer's specification and shielded from moisture, debris, and excessive sunlight. They have sensitive electronics that can wear out from heat, moisture, or excessive use. Batteries are almost always the first part of the system to fail, while inverters and charge controllers tend to be next, no matter how well designed your system may be.

When electronics such as inverters and charge controllers get hot, they usually need fans to run at full speed. This will age the equipment and can cause failures earlier than expected. Fan failure is a common problem for old inverters. Replacing the fan quickly, though, may prevent other problems from over-heated electronics. Either way, you should expect to replace the inverter and the charge controller at year 10.

Below is a list of potential error messages and the applicable troubleshooting techniques for your inverter or charge controller.

DC Under Voltage:
- Check for module shading or soiling on the glass.
- Replace all blown fuses between PV array and inverter.
- Measure voltage and current close to the PV array and then again close to the electronics. If there is a significant difference, check all fuses, conductors, and conductor terminations between those two points.
- Check to see if the MPPT Charge Controller is performing as expected. Measure the voltage and current before and after the charge controller.

DC Over Voltage:
- During the day, with sufficient sunlight, perform a Voc string test. Disconnect the PV array from the charge controller so it is not supplying a load. Measure the voltage at the PV combiner box or at the end of the module string and check to see if voltage exceeds the input of the charge controller or inverter. This is more likely to happen during cold days with intense sunlight.
- If voltage is too high, reduce Voc by changing array angle or reducing the number of modules in a string.

DC Ground Fault:
- Testing for ground fault can be challenging since sometimes a ground fault only happens when the system is wet or at a particular angle.
- Turn off inverter, DC, and AC disconnect. Test the ground fault fuse with an ohmmeter or continuity meter.
- If the fuse is still good, there might not be a ground fault. Test the voltage to ground with the fuse removed. If voltage is low and within specifications, replace fuse and restart inverter.

- If the fuse is not good, then there might be a ground fault. Make sure the fuse is appropriately sized and is the right type. Identify the string that has the ground fault with a voltage meter. If the voltage is close to the Voc of the string, then the fault is likely at the normally grounded end of the string. If the voltage is different, then it is likely in the middle of the array or even in the module.

AC Under/Over Voltage:
- Disconnect all other AC sources, such as a generator or wind turbine.
- Check to see that all the breakers are on and test the AC voltage with a multimeter.
- If it is within range, manually restart the inverter.
- Test again after restart and, if still out of range, call the inverter manufacturer.

Low Power:
- Most likely there is not enough sunlight to initiate the charge controller or inverter. If it is sunny, follow the same procedures as DC Under Voltage above.

Over Heating or High Temperature:
- Test the power supply for the fan. If working, replace the fan motor; otherwise, replace the power supply.
- Clean out the air filters for the intake and the exhaust and make sure the sensor is giving accurate readings.

Software/Firmware Error:
- First try a manual restart, and then try updating the firmware. If the problem persists, call the manufacturer.

Module and Racking Maintenance

Dust covering the modules can greatly reduce the production of the system. If sited in an area without regular rainfall, it is recommended to clean off the modules to improve production. It's best to keep an eye on the array and ensure it is clean, but, at minimum, the modules should be cleaned off once or twice a year. If the modules have a significant tilt, normal rainfall should do a majority of the cleaning for you.

Be careful to not pour cold water on hot modules; the difference in temperature could shock and crack the glass. It's best to clean the modules in the morning or late evening. Never walk on the modules. If you have to walk on them, then only walk on the edges of the frames, stepping near the points of contact with the racking.

Check the racking for signs of daily cycles of thermal expansion. Some racking systems are not designed to handle the daily cycle of expansion and contraction of the metal, glass, and plastic parts. It is possible that wires will creep, clips and attachments could loosen or snap, and hardware could loosen over time. If necessary, retighten hardware and use appropriate adhesive to prevent hardware from slipping.

If ground footings for the racking are getting compromised due to erosion, consider pouring more concrete or using gravel to secure the feet in place.

Understanding Electricity

I saved this chapter for the end of the book since it is such heavy reading. But its placement at the end doesn't mean that it's not important. Understanding electricity as it relates to solar energy systems is critical for a properly functioning system and for your safety.

Below I will explain the basic concepts of electricity required to design and operate an off grid energy system. It is important to develop a complete understanding of each section below. If you don't completely understand all the concepts, then nothing beats hands-on work experience.

Power vs. Energy

People sometimes mistakenly use the words "power" and "energy" interchangeably, not knowing the difference. Power is an instantaneous rate and is the *ratio* of energy per unit of time. By contrast, energy is the *amount* of power that is generated or consumed over a period of time. Solar panels produce *power* when exposed to sunlight and batteries take in that power over time and store the *energy*.

Here is an analogy: within electric cars the batteries need high power for quick acceleration, but they also need plenty of energy capacity to drive long distances. Power is the instantaneous force that allows the car to accelerate quickly, so with low power the car would accelerate slowly. Energy is the capacity or the amount of time the power is available, so with low energy the car could not travel long distances.

What is a watt-hour?

The unit commonly described for energy is a watt-hour (Wh), which is not a ratio. It is not watts per hour; it is watt-hours. I'm referring to the two units — watt and hour – which are in the numerator (top side of the fraction).

$$Wh$$

Here is an example: a light bulb uses a little bit of energy to shine for a second but uses more energy to shine for an hour, even though that light bulb always uses the same amount of power.

How much energy does a light bulb consume? It depends on the power measurement of the light bulb and the length of time it is on. If a 15-watt light bulb is used for 10 hours, it will use 150 watt-hours of energy.

Watts, Voltage, and Amps

Another source of confusion is the relationship of volts, amps, and watts. A watt (W) is also equal to voltage (V) times current (I). So the current flow of one amp with a voltage of one volt is equal to the power of one watt. All of these units are interrelated.

$$Power = Volts \times Amps$$
$$1\,watt = 1\,volt \times 1\,amp$$

After reading, you should understand that power is the ratio of energy per time and energy is either generated or consumed.

Power:
$$1\,watt = 1\,volt \times 1\,amp$$

Energy:
$$1\,watt\,hour = 1\,watt \times hour = 1\,volt \times 1\,amp \times 1\,hour$$

With solar energy systems we will talk about power in watts (W) or kilowatts (kW) and energy in watt-hours (Wh) or kilowatt-hours (kWh).

Voltage and Volts

Voltage is the potential to flow

Voltage is the amount of electric potential and is measured in volts (V). Voltage always measures the difference in electrical potential between two parts of a circuit. It is commonly compared to pressure.

For example, imagine two water buckets: one full of water, the other one empty. If a pipe connects the two near the bottom, the water will rush from the full bucket to the empty bucket, because of the water pressure. The same thing will happen if you connect a solar module and a battery. As long as the solar panel has a higher voltage, or "pressure," it will push energy into the battery.

In a solar energy system, all the components are designed to function within a particular voltage range. Some components could be damaged if they are exposed to a voltage higher than their designed voltage threshold. Be sure to have a strong understanding of the voltage requirements of your equipment before you connect a circuit. For example, charge controllers are designed with a maximum input voltage. Having too many modules attached in series can overload the circuit and cause the electronics to short circuit.

Current and Amperes

Current is the flow

Current, also known as amperage, is the measure of electrical flow and is measured in amperes or amps (A). The conventional symbol is I. You can think of this as the number of electrons moving through a conductor in a given time period. One ampere is literally the measurement of 6 billion billion (6.2415×10^{18}) electrons per second!

In the water bucket analogy, it is like the amount of water flowing per unit of time.

If a circuit has no voltage, then it has no current. Or in other words, if there is no difference in electric potential, then there will be no flow of electricity. In the water bucket analogy, it is like the amount of water flowing per unit of time. When both buckets have the same level of water, there is no potential energy left and the water does not flow anywhere.

What would happen if you filled up one bucket and left the other one empty but then put a valve between the two tanks? There would be no flow of water when the valve was closed. The water has the potential to flow when you open the valve, but, since it is not flowing, there is no current. This example shows us that there can be voltage without current. These examples taken together illustrate the difference between a dead battery and a fully charged one. A fully charged battery that is unplugged has a voltage, or a difference in electric potential. Because it is unplugged, it has no current flow, thus consuming no energy.

Resistance

Electrical **Resistance** is a measure of how much a conductor opposes the passage of electrons. It represents the difficulty of electricity to flow and is measured in Ohms (Ω). The resistance of a conductor is defined as the ratio of voltage across it to current through it. It is common to see a voltage drop during high peaks of current when there is significant resistance, because it resists the flow of current.

It is important to understand resistance as it relates to wire size and wire length. The longer a wire, the higher the resistance. Also, the thinner a wire, the higher the resistance. High resistance turns into heat and heat in your electrical wiring can cause a fire. Resistance can also build up from a damaged wire or a poorly secured connection. If you ever notice an unusually hot wire or extension cord, replace it ASAP.

OHM'S LAW CARTOON

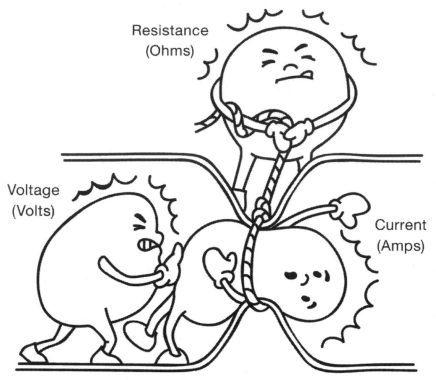

Resistance (Ohms)

Voltage (Volts)

Current (Amps)

Illustration by Jean-Baptiste Vervaeck

Ohm's Law

Now that you have a better understanding of voltage, current, and resistance, let's tie it all together. With solar systems we generally want to be mindful of resistance in our circuit in order to avoid too much of a drop in voltage. Ohm's Law states that the electric potential difference (ΔV) between two points on a circuit is the product of the total current (I) and total resistance (R) between those two points in the circuit.

$$\Delta V = I \times R$$

This equation is frequently used, as it is a predictor of the relationships between voltage drop, current and resistance. All conductors experience some resistance; your goal is to minimize it. As you design your system, Ohm's Law will help determine the acceptable voltage drop. You are in control of the conductor sizing, and must ensure that resistance is kept to a minimum. Otherwise, the conductors can get hot from the increased resistance and cause a fire.

There is a delicate balance between acceptable voltage drop and conductor size. When connecting components in short distances to each other, it's practical to simply use larger-gauge wire than necessary without too much extra cost. But running longer distances can be expensive, as thicker-gauge wire costs more than thinner-gauge wire. This is a case for defining exactly the right gauge of wire for your particular setup using a voltage drop calculator. Also consider the metal used as a conductor, since aluminum physically has more resistance than copper with the same wire profile diameter.

Ohm's Law Formula Wheel

The graphic on the next page shows how power, voltage, current, and resistance are all related. In this graphic, voltage is represented with an E, since the scientific reference to voltage is electromotive force. If you know two variables, this chart helps you find the third. For example, let's say you want to know the maximum current in a circuit if you have an inverter with a maximum output of 1500 W at 120 V. To find the current, you look for "I" on the top left side of the wheel and find the equation below with "P" power and "E" voltage.

$$I = \frac{P}{E} = \frac{1500W}{120V} = 12.5A$$

OHM'S LAW FORMULA WHEEL

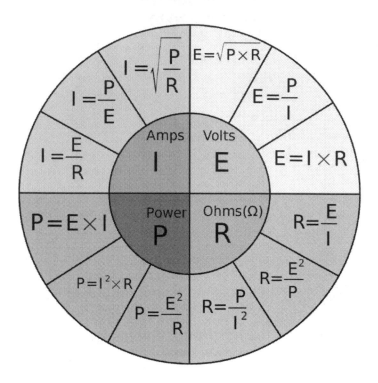

Matt Rider / CC-BY-SA-3.0

More Resources

I encourage you to contact me directly if you still have questions or concerns about the content of this book. This is the second edition of the book, and my goal is to provide all the resources required to design and install an off grid solar energy system anywhere in the world. If there is something particularly challenging in your area of the world, let me know! I encourage you to share your knowledge with me and also with others seeking to learn more about solar energy.

On my website there are more resources available to assist you in the design of an off grid solar system. These resources are free for download:
- System Designer template in MS Excel
    - Load Calculator Table
    - Derate Table
    - System Summary
- Bill of Materials template in MS Excel
- Solar insolation maps
- Declination maps
- Voltage Drop Calculator
- GOGLA *Photovoltaics for Productive Use Applications: A Catalogue of DC-Appliances.*

Please visit the following links to access more information or to contact me about the book.

www.OffGridSolarBook.com

OCON Energy Consulting

As the founder of OCON Energy Consulting, Joe O'Connor provides consulting services for a range of clients in need of solar system design, energy storage systems, and product development. Please visit the following link for more information or to contact OCON Energy about consulting opportunities.

www.OCONEnergy.com

Modular Energy Systems

Joe O'Connor founded Modular Energy Systems (MES), a firm providing high quality, reliable energy storage products that streamline the installation process. MES designs fully-integrated high quality energy systems so the installer doesn't have to spend time and money on design, installation, and service.

MES engineers have built systems for all climate conditions and they understand the needs in extreme weather conditions. Whether addressing extreme low temperatures or hot and humid climates, MES designs systems that provide continuous uninterrupted power.

www.ModEnergySystems.com

Acknowledgements

Thank you Greg Van Kirk, for exposing me to your world and showing me the impact that solar can have on the people of Haiti and Guatemala.

Thank you Benjamin Materna and David Reichbaum, for including me in GivePower Foundation.

I am grateful to have been a part of such a great team during the installation in Virunga National Park. Barrett Raftery, Dan Retz, James Winttuck, Garth Pratt, Dusty Hulet, Rodney Hansen and Sefu Kasali Kibengo Trésor, you guys were the best. I am glad we all had a chance to work together on such an important project.

Thanks for your support on my second edition Matt Sisul and Nate Wennyk. Thank you solar mentors and friends: John Humphrey, Barry Cogbill, Bob Rudd, Rene Kress, Ian Petrich, Randy Bachelor, Michael Worry, Joe Stofega, Lucie Dupas, and especially George Schnakenberg III.

Index

MODBUS · 54

T

Temperature · 28, 53, 64, 70, 89, 97, 153, 177
Temperature coefficient · 90, 158
Temperature compensation · 97
Thermal cycling · 132, 133
Thermal runaway · 49, 50, 52, 59, 70
Tier 1 module · 81
True north · 23, 170

U

Underwriters Laboratories (UL) · 110

V

Volt (V) · viii, 13, 32, 33, 36, 37, 38, 39, 44, 46, 50, 51, 52, 53, 55, 56, 57, 59, 60, 64, 65, 66, 67, 75, 76, 78, 79, 80, 81, 82, 83, 85, 87, 88, 89, 90, 91, 92, 93, 94, 95, 96, 100, 101, 104, 107, 112, 115, 117, 120, 121, 140, 151, 152, 154, 155, 158, 159, 160, 165, 167, 168, 170, 171, 172, 176, 177, 180, 181, 182, 183, 184, 185, 187
Voltage drop · viii, 59, 75, 85, 94, 96, 112, 117, 167, 183, 185, 187
Volts per cell · 171

W

Watt-hour · 14, 16, 18, 28, 64, 160, 180, 181
Watts · 14, 16, 17, 18, 19, 20, 24, 25, 42, 78, 84, 106, 107, 138, 151, 155, 156, 158, 160, 167, 180, 181, 185
Watts per square meter · 24, 84
Wind load · 144, 145
Wind power · 139
Wind turbine · 34, 177
Wire · 32, 57, 67, 100, 102, 104, 109, 110, 111, 112, 113, 114, 115, 116, 117, 118, 120, 122, 126, 132, 133, 134, 158, 161, 162, 164, 165, 173, 183, 185
Aluminum · 109
clip · 132, 133
Copper · 109, 110, 115, 120, 185
gauge · 67, 110, 111, 114, 115, 117, 118
NM · 111, 113, 162
PV · 113, 114, 162
RHH/RHW · 111, 113
Romex · 111, 113, 162
THHN/THWN · 111, 113
type · 67, 110, 113, 114, 164, 165
USE/UF · 111, 113

Y

Y-combiner · 89

Z

Zip tie · 132, 133